Unit Resource Guide
Unit 16

Bringing It All Together:
An Assessment Unit

THIRD EDITION

KENDALL/HUNT PUBLISHING COMPANY
4050 Westmark Drive   Dubuque, Iowa   52002

A TIMS® Curriculum
University of Illinois at Chicago

UIC The University of Illinois
at Chicago

The original edition was based on work supported by the National Science Foundation under grant
No. MDR 9050226 and the University of Illinois at Chicago. Any opinions, findings, and conclusions
or recommendations expressed in this publication are those of the author(s) and do not necessarily
reflect the views of the granting agencies.

Letter Home

Bringing It All Together: An Assessment Unit

Date: _____

Dear Family Member:

In the final unit of fifth grade, your child will reflect on his or her growth in mathematics during this school year. Your child will review the labs, assessment problems, and other activities completed throughout the year.

As part of these end-of-year activities, your child will participate in a lab that simulates a method used by scientists for estimating the population of animals. Students first read a story about scientists estimating the number of bats in a cave. Then they use beans in a bag to represent the bats. After "tagging" (marking) some of the beans, your child will "recapture" the beans by taking several samples from the bag and counting the number of tagged beans in each sample. Then we will use the data to estimate the total number of beans in the bag.

Students will also solve a problem using patterns, then write up their solutions. They will take an end-of-year test. Finally, students will compare the work from this unit with similar activities completed earlier in the year. The work collected in your child's portfolio will document the progress he or she has made in mathematics during the year.

As your child works on these activities in school, you can help at home by encouraging your child to think about the skills and concepts that he or she has learned this year in mathematics class. Ask your child to tell about his or her favorite lab.

Thank you for your help and support during this school year.

Sincerely,

Carta al hogar

Reuniéndolo todo: una unidad de evaluación

Fecha: _____

Estimado miembro de familia:

En la última unidad de quinto grado, su hijo/a tendrá la oportunidad de reflexionar acerca de su avance en las matemáticas durante este año escolar.

Su hijo/a repasará las investigaciones de laboratorio, los problemas de evaluación y otras actividades completadas durante el año.

Como parte de estas actividades de fin de año, su hijo/a participará en una experiencia de laboratorio que simula un método que usan los científicos para estimar el tamaño de una población de animales. Los estudiantes primero leerán un cuento acerca de científicos que estiman el número de murciélagos en una cueva. Luego, usarán frijoles de una bolsa para representar los murciélagos. Después de marcar algunos de los frijoles, su hijo/a volverá a "capturar" los frijoles tomando varias muestras de la bolsa y contando el número de frijoles marcados en cada muestra. Luego, usaremos los datos para estimar el número total de frijoles en la bolsa.

Los estudiantes también resolverán un problema usando patrones y anotarán las soluciones. Tendrán luego un examen de fin de año. Por último, los estudiantes compararán el trabajo hecho en esta unidad con actividades semejantes completadas anteriormente durante el año. El trabajo reunido en el portafolio de su hijo/a documentará el avance en las matemáticas durante el año.

Mientras su hijo/a trabaja sobre estas actividades en la escuela, usted le puede ayudar en casa animándole a que piense en habilidades y conceptos que ha aprendido este año en la clase de matemáticas. Pídale a su hijo/a que le cuente sobre su experiencia de laboratorio favorita.

Gracias por la ayuda y el apoyo que nos ha dado durante este año escolar.

Atentamente,

_____

Table of Contents

Unit 16
Bringing It All Together: An Assessment Unit

Unit 16

Outline

Bringing It All Together: An Assessment Unit

Unit Summary

Estimated Class Sessions
10-12

This unit reviews, extends, and assesses the concepts students studied throughout the year. Students revisit the labs they completed during the year in preparation for completing an assessment lab. This lab is based on the Adventure Book *Bats!* in which a family helps a scientist estimate the number of bats in a cave. In the lab *How Many Bats in a Cave?* students use beans in a container to model the sampling procedures used in the story.

Using a similar procedure and proportional reasoning, students estimate the number of beans in their containers. Students also use pattern blocks to solve an assessment problem, *Pattern Block Candy.* Finally, students take an *End-of-Year Test,* which assesses concepts from Units 13–15. The unit ends with a review of students' portfolios.

Major Concept Focus

- experiment review
- *Adventure Book:* estimating animal populations
- populations and samples
- TIMS Laboratory Method
- point graphs
- ratios and proportions
- communicating solution strategies
- best-fit lines
- using data to solve problems
- Student Rubric: *Solving*
- end-of-year test
- portfolio review

Pacing Suggestions

This unit will take 10 to 12 days to complete. It includes a variety of review and assessment activities that provide opportunities for teachers to assess individual growth in mathematics as students apply concepts and skills in new contexts.

- Lesson 2 *Bats!* is an *Adventure Book* story that provides a strong connection to language arts, social studies, and science. It sets the stage for the assessment lab in Lesson 4 *How Many Bats in a Cave?* It is appropriate to use language arts or science time for students to read and discuss the story.
- Lesson 3 *More Bats!* and Lesson 4 *How Many Bats in a Cave?* provide connections to science. Students can collect the data for the lab in Lesson 4 during science time.

Assessment Indicators

Use the following Assessment Indicators and the *Observational Assessment Record* that follows the Background section in this unit to assess students on key ideas.

A1. Can students collect, organize, graph, and analyze data?

A2. Can students draw and interpret best-fit lines?

A3. Can students translate between graphs and real-world events?

A4. Can students use words, tables, graphs, and fractions to express ratios?

A5. Can students use ratios and proportions to solve problems?

A6. Can students use numerical variables?

A7. Can students identify and describe number patterns?

A8. Can students solve open-response problems and communicate solution strategies?

A9. Do students solve problems in more than one way?

Unit Planner

	Lesson Information	Supplies	Copies/ Transparencies
Lesson 1 **Experiment Review** URG Pages 22–32 SG Page 488 DAB Pages 235–237 DPP A–D HP Part 1 *Estimated Class Sessions* **2**	**Activity** Students review the labs they worked on during the past year by recounting the important features of each lab. The class discusses the similarities and differences between the labs. **Homework** Assign Part 1 of the Home Practice.	• portfolios	• 1 transparency of *Comparing Lives of Animals and Soap Bubbles Lab* URG Page 30 • 1 transparency of *Experiment Review Chart* DAB Pages 235–237 or a large sheet of easel paper for a class chart
Lesson 2 **Bats!** URG Pages 33–42 AB Pages 93–106 DPP E–F HP Part 2 *Estimated Class Sessions* **1**	**Adventure Book** Students read a story about using a capture-recapture technique to estimate the size of a bat population in a cave. The story describes how scientists collected the data and used proportional reasoning to calculate an estimate. **Math Facts** DPP item E provides practice with division facts. **Homework** 1. Assign DPP Challenge F, which explores mass, volume, and density. 2. Assign Part 2 of the Home Practice, which reviews fractions, decimals, and percents.	• map of the United States, optional	
Lesson 3 **More Bats!** URG Pages 43–50 SG Pages 489–491 AB Pages 93–106 DPP G–H *Estimated Class Sessions* **1**	**Activity** Students expand on the story *Bats!* as they graph the data collected by a conservation club. This lesson reviews skills needed for Lesson 4. **Math Facts** Complete DPP item G, which reviews the division facts. **Assessment** Use the *Observational Assessment Record* to note students' abilities to express ratios using words, tables, graphs, and fractions.	• 1 calculator per student • 1 ruler per student	• 1 copy of *Centimeter Graph Paper* URG Page 49 per student • 1 copy of *Observational Assessment Record* URG Pages 9–10 to be used throughout this unit

	Lesson Information	Supplies	Copies/ Transparencies
Lesson 4 **How Many Bats in a Cave?** URG Pages 51–66 SG Pages 492–497 DPP I–N HP Parts 3–4 *Estimated Class Sessions* **3**	**Assessment Lab** Using beans to represent bats in a cave, students simulate the capture-recapture technique described in the Adventure Book *Bats!* Using this technique and proportional reasoning, students find the approximate number of "bats" in their "cave." **Math Facts** Assign DPP item I, which reviews the division facts. **Homework** 1. Assign the homework in the *Student Guide*. Students will need a piece of *Centimeter Graph Paper*. 2. Assign Parts 3 and 4 of the Home Practice. **Assessment** Choose one or more sections of the lab to use as an assessment.	• brightly colored markers for tagging the beans per student group • 1 self-closing bag filled with 1 lb. of baby lima beans per student group • 3 sizes of scoops: small (about 2 tablespoons), medium (about 4 tablespoons), and large (about 6 tablespoons) per student group • 1 ruler per student • 1 calculator per student	• 1 copy of *Three-column Data Table* URG Page 63 per student, optional • 2 copies of *Centimeter Graph Paper* URG Page 49 per student • 1 transparency of *Centimeter Graph Paper* URG Page 49, optional • 1 copy of *TIMS Multidimensional Rubric* TIG Assessment section, optional
Lesson 5 **Pattern Block Candy** URG Pages 67–78 DPP O–P HP Part 5 *Estimated Class Sessions* **1-2**	**Assessment Activity** Students use pattern blocks to build patterns. Using the *Solving* Rubric, they use the patterns to solve problems and then write about their solutions. **Math Facts** Complete DPP item O, which reviews the division facts. **Homework** Assign Part 5 of the Home Practice. **Assessment** Use the *TIMS Multidimensional Rubric* to score students' work. Encourage students to compare their work on this activity to similar activities in their portfolios.	• 1 calculator per student • 1 set of pattern blocks (4 or 5 of each shape: red trapezoid, blue rhombus, green triangle, brown trapezoid, purple triangle) per student	• 1 copy of *Pattern Block Candy* URG Pages 76–77 per student • 1 transparency or poster of Student Rubric: *Solving* TIG Assessment section, optional • 1 copy of *TIMS Multidimensional Rubric* TIG Assessment section, optional
Lesson 6 **End-of-Year Test** URG Pages 79–91 DPP Q–R HP Part 6 *Estimated Class Sessions* **1-2**	**Assessment Activity** Students complete a short item test designed to assess skills and concepts learned during the final quarter of the year. **Assessment** 1. Students solve the problems on the *End-of-Year Test* using tools available to them in the classroom. 2. Assign Part 6 of the Home Practice.	• 1 ruler per student • 1 protractor per student • 1 compass per student • 1 calculator per student	• 1 copy of *End-of-Year Test* URG Pages 83–87 per student • 1 copy of *Centimeter Dot Paper* URG Page 88 per student

(Continued)

	Lesson Information	Supplies	Copies/Transparencies
Lesson 7 **Portfolio Review** URG Pages 92–96 SG Pages 498–499 DPP S–T *Estimated Class Sessions* **1**	**Assessment Activity** Students review their portfolios, looking at their growth since the start of the school year. **Math Facts** Complete DPP item S, which involves finding a pattern in a data table and continuing it. **Assessment** Transfer appropriate documentation from the Unit 16 *Observational Assessment Record* to students' *Individual Assessment Record Sheets*.	• collection folders • portfolio folders	• 1 copy of *Individual Assessment Record Sheet* TIG Assessment section per student, previously copied for use throughout the year

Connections

A current list of literature and software connections is available at *www.mathtrailblazers.com*. You can also find information on connections in the *Teacher Implementation Guide* Literature List and Software List sections.

Literature Connections
Suggested Titles
- Barbour and Davis. *Bats of America.* Books on Demand, Ann Arbor, MI, 1994.
- Cannon, Janell. *Stellaluna.* Harcourt Brace & Company, Orlando, FL, 1993. (Lesson 4)
- Lovett, Sara. *Extremely Weird Bats.* Avalon Travel Publishing, Emeryville, CA, 2002.

Software Connections
- Bandelier National Monument World Wide Web site (http://www.nps.gov/band/). Provides information for visitors to Bandelier National Monument including location, hours, and fees. There is also some specific information about climate, activities, and accessibility.
- Bat Conservation International World Wide Web site (http://www.batcon.org/). Comprehensive web site dedicated to the conservation of bats. It includes bat activities, facts, and trivia as well as links to other bat sites and information about bat workshops and museum exhibits.
- *Graph Master* allows students to collect data and create their own graphs.
- *TinkerPlots* allows students to record, compare, and analyze data in tables and graphs.

Teaching All Math Trailblazers Students

Math Trailblazers® lessons are designed for students with a wide range of abilities. The lessons are flexible and do not require significant adaptation for diverse learning styles or academic levels. However, when needed, lessons can be tailored to allow students to engage their abilities to the greatest extent possible while building knowledge and skills.

To assist you in meeting the needs of all students in your classroom, this section contains information about some of the features in the curriculum that allow all students access to mathematics. For additional information, see the Teaching the *Math Trailblazers* Student: Meeting Individual Needs section in the *Teacher Implementation Guide.*

Differentiation Opportunities in this Unit

Laboratory Experiments

Laboratory experiments enable students to solve problems using a variety of representations including pictures, tables, graphs, and symbols. Teachers can assign or adapt parts of the analysis according to the student's ability. The following lesson is a lab:

- Lesson 4 *How Many Bats in a Cave?*

Journal Prompts

Journal prompts provide opportunities for students to explain and reflect on mathematical problems. They can help both students who need practice explaining their ideas and students who benefit from answering higher order questions. Students with various learning styles can express themselves using pictures, words, and sentences. Teachers can alter journal prompts to suit students' ability levels. The following lessons contain a journal prompt:

- Lesson 1 *Experiment Review*
- Lesson 5 *Pattern Block Candy*

DPP Challenges

DPP Challenges are items from the Daily Practice and Problems that usually take more than fifteen minutes to complete. These problems are more thought-provoking and can be used to stretch students' problem-solving skills. The following lessons have DPP Challenges in them:

- DPP Challenge D from Lesson 1 *Experiment Review*
- DPP Challenge F from Lesson 2 *Bats!*
- DPP Challenge H from Lesson 3 *More Bats!*
- DPP Challenge N from Lesson 4 *How Many Bats in a Cave?*

Extensions

Use extensions to enrich lessons. Many extensions provide opportunities to further involve or challenge students of all abilities. Take a moment to review the extensions prior to beginning this unit. Some extensions may require additional preparation and planning. The following lesson contains an extension:

- Lesson 4 *How Many Bats in a Cave?*

Unit 16

Background
Bringing It All Together:
An Assessment Unit

Since this unit concludes the school year, the lessons review, extend, and assess concepts students learned throughout the year. Because the activities in this unit are similar to those in other assessment units, you can compare students' work to their work on similar tasks. For example, in the problem-solving task, *Pattern Block Candy,* students solve a problem and then communicate their solution strategies. You can compare their work on this task to their work on other assessment problems such as *Stack Up* in Unit 2 and *Florence Kelley's Report* in Unit 8.

Students also revisit each of the labs they completed during the year. This review provides an opportunity for students to reinforce key concepts learned from the labs. After students complete the assessment lab, *How Many Bats in a Cave?*, you can compare their work to their work on any labs completed during the year. This will help you assess their progress in gathering, organizing, displaying, and analyzing data. A short item test covering skills and concepts from Units 13, 14, 15, and 16 is also included. At the end of the unit, students have an opportunity to review and add to their portfolios. The assessments in this unit, combined with the information gathered through daily observations, result in a balanced assessment of each student's growth.

Resources

- *Assessment Standards for School Mathematics.* National Council of Teachers of Mathematics, Reston, VA, 1995.
- Barbour and Davis. *Bats of America.* Books on Demand, Ann Arbor, MI, 1994.
- Phillips, Elizabeth, et al. *Understanding Rational Numbers and Proportions* from the Curriculum and Evaluation Standards Addenda Series, Grades 5–8. National Council of Teachers of Mathematics, Reston, VA, 1994.
- Stenmark, J.K. (ed.) *Mathematics Assessment: Myths, Models, Good Questions, and Practical Suggestions.* National Council of Teachers of Mathematics, Reston, VA, 1991.

Observational Assessment Record

A1 Can students collect, organize, graph, and analyze data?

A2 Can students draw and interpret best-fit lines?

A3 Can students translate between graphs and real-world events?

A4 Can students use words, tables, graphs, and fractions to express ratios?

A5 Can students use ratios and proportions to solve problems?

A6 Can students use numerical variables?

A7 Can students identify and describe number patterns?

A8 Can students solve open-response problems and communicate solution strategies?

A9 Do students solve problems in more than one way?

A10 _____

Name	A1	A2	A3	A4	A5	A6	A7	A8	A9	A10	Comments
1.											
2.											
3.											
4.											
5.											
6.											
7.											
8.											
9.											
10.											
11.											
12.											
13.											

Name	A1	A2	A3	A4	A5	A6	A7	A8	A9	A10	Comments
14.											
15.											
16.											
17.											
18.											
19.											
20.											
21.											
22.											
23.											
24.											
25.											
26.											
27.											
28.											
29.											
30.											
31.											
32.											

Unit 16

Daily Practice and Problems

Bringing It All Together:
An Assessment Unit

A DPP Menu for Unit 16

Two Daily Practice and Problems (DPP) items are included for each class session listed in the Unit Outline. A scope and sequence chart for the DPP is in the *Teacher Implementation Guide*.

Icons in the Teacher Notes column designate the subject matter of each DPP item. The first item in each class session is always a Bit and the second is either a Task or Challenge. Each item falls into one or more of the categories listed below. A menu of the DPP items for Unit 16 follows.

N	Number Sense	⊠	Computation	⏰	Time	◫	Geometry
	A, C, D, J, L, P, Q, S, T		A, B, J, L–N, P, T				H, K, R

$\frac{5}{\times 7}$	Math Facts	$	Money	ⵜ	Measurement	◪	Data
	E, G, I, O, S		L, N		F, H, K, R		C

The *Daily Practice and Problems and Home Practice Guide* in the *Teacher Implementation Guide* includes information on how and when to use the DPP.

Review and Assessment of Math Facts

The DPP for this unit reviews the related division facts for all five groups of multiplication facts (2s and 3s, 5s and 10s, square numbers, 9s, and the last six facts—4×6, 4×7, 4×8, 6×7, 6×8, and 7×8).

For more information about the distribution and assessment of the math facts, see the TIMS Tutor: *Math Facts* in the *Teacher Implementation Guide*. Also, refer to Unit 2 Lesson Guide 2 and the DPP guide in the *Unit Resource Guide* for Unit 2. For information about division fact practice through-out second semester, see the DPP guide for Unit 9.

Daily Practice and Problems

Students may solve the items individually, in groups, or as a class. The items may also be assigned for homework. The DPPs are also available on the Teacher Resource CD.

Student Questions	Teacher Notes

A Making Brownies

Below is Blanca's favorite brownie recipe.

$\frac{1}{2}$ cup butter   2 cups flour

$1\frac{1}{2}$ cups sugar $\frac{3}{4}$ cup chocolate syrup

4 eggs   1 cup chocolate chips

$\frac{1}{4}$ tsp. vanilla $\frac{1}{3}$ cup walnuts

1. Blanca likes to double the amount of vanilla, chocolate syrup, and walnuts. How much of each should she add?

2. Blanca uses equal amounts of brown sugar and white sugar. If she needs a total of $1\frac{1}{2}$ cups of sugar, how much of each type of sugar should she use?

TIMS Bit

1. vanilla: $\frac{1}{2}$ tsp.;
   syrup: $1\frac{1}{2}$ cups;
   walnuts: $\frac{2}{3}$ cup
2. $\frac{3}{4}$ cup brown sugar
   and $\frac{3}{4}$ cup white sugar

B Computation

Use an appropriate tool to find an exact answer for each of the following problems. Mental math, paper and pencil, or calculators may be appropriate. Tell which tool you used to solve each problem.

Estimate to see if your answers are reasonable.

A. $6400 \div 80 =$ B. $20 \times 400 =$

C. $8525 \div 25 =$ D. $1855 \div 5 =$

E. $254 \times 589 =$ F. $41{,}862 \div 12 =$

TIMS Task

Strategies may vary.

Mental math is appropriate for A and B.

A. 80   B. 8000

Paper and pencil is an appropriate strategy for C and D.

C. 341   D. 371

Calculators are appropriate for E and F.

E. 149,606   F. 3488.5

Student Questions	Teacher Notes

C Favorite Pets

John took a survey in his neighborhood. He asked the neighbors on his block to choose one animal as their favorite type of pet. He displayed the results in this circle graph. Use the circle graph to answer the questions below.

Favorite Pets

- 44% Cat
- 3% Bird
- 13% Guinea Pig
- 27% Dog
- 4% Rabbit
- 9% Fish

1. What percent of his neighbors like cats the best?

2. What percent of his neighbors like birds, fish, or guinea pigs?

3. What percent of his neighbors did not choose dogs as their favorite?

TIMS Bit [N] [graph icon]

1. 44%
2. 25%
3. 73%

D Factors

Which numbers from 1 to 100 have the most factors?

TIMS Challenge [N]

60, 72, 84, 90, and 96 all have 12 factors.

Student Questions	Teacher Notes

 Division Fact Practice

A. 50 ÷ 5 =

B. 12 ÷ 3 =

C. 90 ÷ 10 =

D. 8 ÷ 2 =

E. 24 ÷ 8 =

F. 28 ÷ 7 =

G. 56 ÷ 8 =

H. 80 ÷ 8 =

I. 4 ÷ 2 =

J. 48 ÷ 8 =

TIMS Bit [5 x7]

A. 10	B. 4
C. 9	D. 4
E. 3	F. 4
G. 7	H. 10
I. 2	J. 6

F Different Densities

Lee Yah and Frank found the mass of 30 cc of vegetable oil and 30 cc of corn syrup. They found that the mass of the vegetable oil is 27 grams and the mass of the corn syrup is 41 grams.

1. Which is denser, vegetable oil or corn syrup? How do you know?

2. Predict what will happen if vegetable oil, water, and corn syrup are poured into the same container. Which liquid will float to the top? Which will sink to the bottom? Draw a picture showing the 3 liquids in the container.

3. Frank finds the mass of a plastic sphere to be 10 g and the volume to be 8.5 cc.

   A. If the sphere is placed in corn syrup, will it sink or float?

   B. If the sphere is placed in vegetable oil, will it sink or float?

TIMS Challenge

1. corn syrup. Responses will vary. One possible response: corn syrup: $\frac{41\,g}{30\,cc}$ gives a density of about 1.4 g/cc. vegetable oil: $\frac{27\,g}{30\,cc}$ gives a density of 0.9 g/cc.

2. The corn syrup will sink and the oil will float. The density of water is 1 g/cc. Since the syrup is denser than water, it will sink to the bottom. The oil is less dense than water, so it will float to the top. A layer of water will separate the syrup and the oil.

3. A. The plastic sphere will float in the syrup since 1.2 g/cc is less than 1.4 g/cc.

   B. The sphere will sink in the oil since 1.2 g/cc is greater than 0.9 g/cc.

G Division Fact Practice

A. $40 \div 10 = n$ B. $n \div 5 = 4$

C. $49 \div n = 7$ D. $27 \div n = 3$

E. $72 \div n = 9$ F. $21 \div 3 = n$

G. $n \div 8 = 2$ H. $n \div 5 = 8$

I. $100 \div 10 = n$ J. $9 \div 3 = n$

K. $n \div 2 = 5$ L. $42 \div n = 7$

TIMS Bit

A. 4   B. 20

C. 7   D. 9

E. 8   F. 7

G. 16   H. 40

I. 10   J. 3

K. 10   L. 6

H The Box Collection

Irma has four new boxes to add to her box collection, which she displays at home in the living room. She places a piece of felt beneath each box so it does not scratch her mother's coffee table. She begins with a rectangular piece of felt that measures 8 inches by 16 inches. She cuts a square off each corner of the felt. She needs two squares that are 4 inches on a side, a square that is 3 inches on a side, and a square that is 2 inches on a side.

1. How much felt will she have left?

2. Draw the piece of felt on a piece of *Centimeter Grid Paper.* Show the squares Irma is cutting out. Find the perimeter of the remaining piece of felt.

TIMS Challenge

1. The area of the felt is 128 square inches. She is cutting off 45 square inches ($4 \times 4 = 16$ sq inches; $16 \times 2 = 32$ sq inches; $3 \times 3 = 9$ square inches; $2 \times 2 = 4$ square inches). She will have 83 square inches left.

2. Answers will vary. One solution is shown below. The perimeter of the remaining piece of felt in this situation is 40 inches.

Student Questions	Teacher Notes

1   Division Fact Practice

A. $36 \div 6 =$

B. $180 \div 20 =$

C. $300 \div 50 =$

D. $3000 \div 100 =$

E. $160 \div 40 =$

F. $36{,}000 \div 400 =$

G. $450 \div 90 =$

H. $1200 \div 60 =$

I. $18{,}000 \div 600 =$

J. $81{,}000 \div 90 =$

K. $630 \div 90 =$

L. $60{,}000 \div 6 =$

TIMS Bit $\boxed{\begin{smallmatrix} 5 \\ \times\, 7 \end{smallmatrix}}$

A. 6
B. 9
C. 6
D. 30
E. 4
F. 90
G. 5
H. 20
I. 30
J. 900
K. 7
L. 10,000

J   Practice

Solve the following using mental math or paper and pencil. Estimate to be sure your answers are reasonable.

A. $48 \times 28 =$

B. $280 \times 7 =$

C. $3006 \div 6 =$

D. $3.4 \times 0.14 =$

E. $7819 \div 46 =$

F. $57.83 + 213.77 =$

TIMS Task   ▨ N

A. 1344
B. 1960
C. 501
D. 0.476
E. 169 R45
F. 271.60

Student Questions	Teacher Notes

K Finding Area

1. What is the area of a triangle whose base is 8 cm and height is 8 cm?

2. If the height is doubled, what is the area?

3. If the height is tripled, what is the area?

1. 32 sq cm
2. 64 sq cm
3. 96 sq cm

L In Proportion

Solve the following. Explain your solutions.

1. If a hotel charges $270 for a 6-night stay, how much is a 2-night stay?

2. If I walk half a mile in ten minutes, how far can I walk in one hour?

3. For every eight children on a field trip there needs to be one adult chaperone. If there are 136 students going on the trip, how many chaperones are needed?

4. For every $20 the students collect in the school fundraiser, $5 goes toward decorating the cafeteria. If $1315 went toward the decoration project, how much money was collected in all?

TIMS Task

1. $90
2. 3 miles
3. 17 chaperones
4. $5260

M Fractions

Use mental math or paper and pencil to solve the following.

A. $5\frac{7}{10} + 3\frac{1}{5} =$

B. $7\frac{4}{5} + 3\frac{1}{4} =$

C. $\frac{1}{2} - \frac{4}{9} =$

D. $1\frac{1}{2} + 2\frac{1}{4} =$

TIMS Bit

A. $8\frac{9}{10}$

B. $11\frac{1}{20}$

C. $\frac{1}{18}$

D. $3\frac{3}{4}$

N Carnival

Admission to the carnival is $2. Then every ride costs 50 cents.

1. Manny and his two brothers together spent $24. They each rode the same number of rides. How many rides did each of the boys go on?

2. Lee Yah does not have to pay the admission fee since she is working a game booth. If she spends $4 on rides, how many rides did she go on?

3. Blanca started with $10. She spent some of her money on rides. She also tried her hand at a ring toss game. It costs $1 for 5 rings. Blanca tossed 15 rings. She now has $4.50 left.

   A. How many rides has Blanca already gone on?

   B. If she wants to buy popcorn for $0.75 and then go on more rides, how many more rides can she go on?

TIMS Challenge

1. 12 rides; they spent $6 on admission leaving $18 or $6 each for rides.

2. 8 rides

3. A. 1 ride; she spent $2 on admission and $3 for the ring toss for a total of $5. She spent 50¢ on one ride.

   B. 7 rides; she will have 25¢ left over.

	Student Questions	Teacher Notes

◎ Division Fact Practice

A. $6 \div 3 = n$ B. $25 \div 5 = n$

C. $n \div 3 = 9$ D. $20 \div n = 10$

E. $24 \div n = 4$ F. $n \div 8 = 8$

G. $54 \div 9 = n$ H. $15 \div 5 = n$

I. $n \div 4 = 8$ J. $n \div 10 = 7$

K. $14 \div n = 2$ L. $35 \div n = 7$

Ⓟ Function Machines

Complete the tables.

$q = (p-2) \div 9$		$s = (r-10) \div 7$		$u = (t+1) \div 4$	
p	q	r	s	t	u
92			9	31	
83		59		27	
	7	52			5
47		38		15	
	3	24			3
	1	17		7	

TIMS Task

$q=(p-2)\div 9$		$s=(r-10)\div 7$		$u=(t+1)\div 4$	
p	q	r	s	t	u
92	10	73	9	31	8
83	9	59	7	27	7
65	7	52	6	19	5
47	5	38	4	15	4
29	3	24	2	11	3
11	1	17	1	7	2

Ⓠ More Bats in the Cave

In their investigation *How Many Bats in a Cave?*, Jeff and Kelly found that about 1 out of every 8 beans in a sample was tagged. If there were 200 tagged beans in their bag, estimate the total number of beans in their bag.

TIMS Bit

1600 beans

| | Student Questions | Teacher Notes |

R Geometry Riddles

1. The perimeter of a rectangle is 48 cm. Its length is 8 cm. What is its area?

2. The sum of the length and width of a rectangle is 10 cm. The area of the rectangle is 24 sq cm. What are the length and width of the rectangle?

TIMS Task

1. 16 cm × 8 cm or 128 sq cm; (48 cm − 8 cm × 2 = 32 cm; 32 ÷ 2 = 16 cm; The width is 16 cm.)

2. Possible lengths and widths to get a sum of 10: 1 and 9; 2 and 8; 3 and 7; 4 and 6; 5 and 5. Since only 4 × 6 = 24, 4 cm and 6 cm are the dimensions of the rectangle.

S Mental Math

Use mental math and patterns to complete the following table. Tell the rule for the table.

Input	Output
0	1
1	6
2	11
	21
7	
11	
	26

TIMS Bit

$n \times 5 + 1$

Input	Output
0	1
1	6
2	11
4	21
7	36
11	56
5	26

Student Questions

T Peanut Butter Cookies

Here are the ingredients for a peanut butter cookie recipe.

$\frac{3}{4}$ cup brown sugar

$\frac{3}{4}$ cup white sugar

1 cup peanut butter

$\frac{1}{3}$ cup shortening

$\frac{1}{3}$ cup butter

$\frac{1}{2}$ tsp. baking powder

1 tsp. baking soda

2 eggs

$2\frac{1}{2}$ cups flour

1 tsp. vanilla

1. It's Arti's birthday. She wants to bring cookies to school. She needs to double the ingredients to make two batches of cookies. List each ingredient and how much Arti needs of each.

2. If the recipe is tripled, how much of each ingredient will Arti need?

Teacher Notes

TIMS Task

N

1. $1\frac{1}{2}$ cups brown sugar and white sugar, 2 cups peanut butter, $\frac{2}{3}$ cup shortening and butter, 1 tsp. baking powder, 2 tsp. baking soda and vanilla, 4 eggs, and 5 cups flour.
2. $2\frac{1}{4}$ cups brown sugar and white sugar, 3 cups peanut butter, 1 cup shortening and butter, $1\frac{1}{2}$ tsp. baking powder, 3 tsp. baking soda and vanilla, 6 eggs, and $7\frac{1}{2}$ cups flour.

Experiment Review

Lesson Overview

Estimated Class Sessions

2

Students review the labs they worked on during the past year by recounting various elements of each lab: variables, number of trials, type of graph, and problems solved. They use work collected in their portfolios and the *Student Guide* to recall each lab. The class discusses the differences and similarities of the experiments.

Key Content

- Comparing and contrasting the following elements of different experiments:

  measurement procedures

  number of trials

  problems solved

  types of graphs

  variables

Key Vocabulary

- bar graph
- point graph
- trial
- variable

Homework

Assign Part 1 of the Home Practice.

Curriculum Sequence

Before This Unit

Students completed a similar activity recalling labs completed in the first semester of fifth grade in Unit 8. If students placed their *Experiment Review Charts* from Unit 8 in their portfolios, they can use them to help complete the new chart for all the labs they completed in fifth grade.

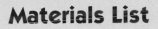

Supplies and Copies

Student	Teacher
Supplies for Each Student • portfolios	**Supplies**
Copies	**Copies/Transparencies** • 1 transparency of *Comparing Lives of Animals and Soap Bubbles Lab* (*Unit Resource Guide* Page 30) • 1 transparency of *Experiment Review Chart* or a large sheet of easel paper for a class chart (*Discovery Assignment Book* Pages 235–237)

All blackline masters including assessment, transparency, and DPP masters are also on the Teacher Resource CD.

Student Books

Experiment Review (*Student Guide* Page 488)
Experiment Review Chart (*Discovery Assignment Book* Pages 235–237)

Daily Practice and Problems and Home Practice

DPP items A–D (*Unit Resource Guide* Pages 12–13)
Home Practice Part 1 (*Discovery Assignment Book* Page 231)

Note: Classrooms whose pacing differs significantly from the suggested pacing of the units should use the Math Facts Calendar in Section 4 of the *Facts Resource Guide* to ensure students receive the complete math facts program.

Daily Practice and Problems

Suggestions for using the DPPs are on page 28.

A. Bit: Making Brownies (URG p. 12)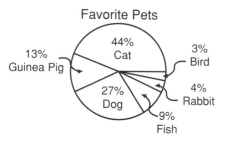

Below is Blanca's favorite brownie recipe.

$\frac{1}{2}$ cup butter   2 cups flour

$1\frac{1}{2}$ cups sugar $\frac{3}{4}$ cup chocolate syrup

4 eggs   1 cup chocolate chips

$\frac{1}{4}$ tsp. vanilla $\frac{1}{3}$ cup walnuts

1. Blanca likes to double the amount of vanilla, chocolate syrup, and walnuts. How much of each should she add?
2. Blanca uses equal amounts of brown sugar and white sugar. If she needs a total of $1\frac{1}{2}$ cups of sugar, how much of each type of sugar should she use?

B. Task: Computation (URG p. 12)

Use an appropriate tool to find an exact answer for each of the following problems. Mental math, paper and pencil, or calculators may be appropriate. Tell which tool you used to solve each problem.

Estimate to see if your answers are reasonable.

A. $6400 \div 80 =$ B. $20 \times 400 =$

C. $8525 \div 25 =$ D. $1855 \div 5 =$

E. $254 \times 589 =$ F. $41,862 \div 12 =$

C. Bit: Favorite Pets (URG p. 13)

John took a survey in his neighborhood. He asked the neighbors on his block to choose one animal as their favorite type of pet. He displayed the results in this circle graph. Use the circle graph to answer the questions below.

Favorite Pets

44% Cat
3% Bird
4% Rabbit
9% Fish
27% Dog
13% Guinea Pig

1. What percent of his neighbors like cats the best?
2. What percent of his neighbors like birds, fish, or guinea pigs?
3. What percent of his neighbors did not choose dogs as their favorite?

D. Challenge: Factors (URG p. 13)

Which numbers from 1 to 100 have the most factors?

The opening paragraph of the *Experiment Review* Activity Page in the *Student Guide* begins a class discussion reviewing the labs completed during the year. Professor Peabody is reminded of the lab *Comparing Lives of Animals and Soap Bubbles* from Unit 8 as he watches students blow bubbles *(Question 1).*

TIMS Tip

Since students reviewed the labs in Units 1–7 in the *Experiment Review* in Unit 8, you may choose to review only the labs in Units 8–15 in this lesson. These labs are: *Comparing Lives of Animals* and *Soap Bubbles* in Unit 8, *Mass vs. Volume* in Unit 13, and *Circumference vs. Diameter* in Unit 14.

During this activity, the class will list the labs they completed in fifth grade. Then, assign each lab to a group of students for review. Begin the review with a whole-class discussion of the lab *Comparing Lives of Animals and Soap Bubbles* using **Question 2** as a

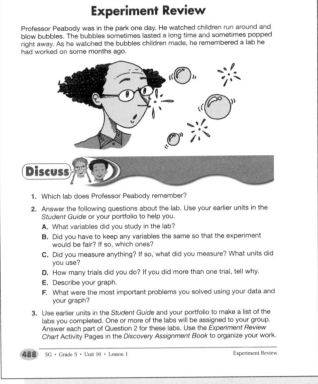

Experiment Review

Professor Peabody was in the park one day. He watched children run around and blow bubbles. The bubbles sometimes lasted a long time and sometimes popped right away. As he watched the bubbles children made, he remembered a lab he had worked on some months ago.

Discuss

1. Which lab does Professor Peabody remember?
2. Answer the following questions about the lab. Use your earlier units in the *Student Guide* or your portfolio to help you.
   A. What variables did you study in the lab?
   B. Did you have to keep any variables the same so that the experiment would be fair? If so, which ones?
   C. Did you measure anything? If so, what did you measure? What units did you use?
   D. How many trials did you do? If you did more than one trial, tell why.
   E. Describe your graph.
   F. What were the most important problems you solved using your data and your graph?
3. Use earlier units in the *Student Guide* and your portfolio to make a list of the labs you completed. One or more of the labs will be assigned to your group. Answer each part of Question 2 for these labs. Use the *Experiment Review Chart* Activity Pages in the *Discovery Assignment Book* to organize your work.

488 SG • Grade 5 • Unit 16 • Lesson 1   Experiment Review

Student Guide - page 488 (Answers on p. 31)

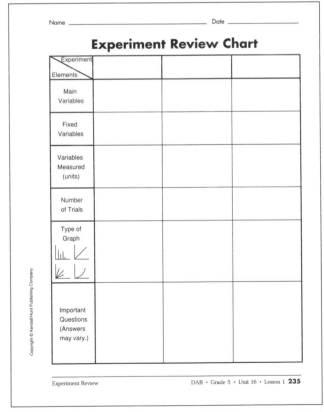

Discovery Assignment Book - page 235 (Answers on p. 32)

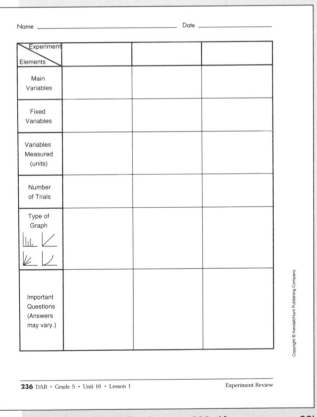

Discovery Assignment Book - page 236 (Answers on p. 32)

guide. A Transparency Master of a sample graph for *Comparing Lives of Animals and Soap Bubbles* has been provided to help you review the lab.

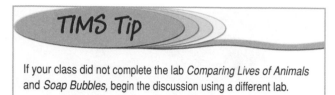

TIMS Tip

If your class did not complete the lab *Comparing Lives of Animals and Soap Bubbles,* begin the discussion using a different lab.

Question 3 asks students to use their portfolios and *Student Guides* to list all the labs they remember working on during the year. After completing this discussion, assign each group of students one or two labs to review using **Question 2** as their guide. The

Experiment Review Chart Activity Pages in the *Discovery Assignment Book* help organize the review information. This chart can then be used to compare and contrast each experiment.

When all groups complete their reviews, each group should report to the class. You can organize the information on a class chart using large chart paper or transparencies of the *Experiment Review Chart,* as shown in Figure 1. Note that the sample responses to **Question 2** for *Comparing Lives of Animals and Soap Bubbles* are shown in the seventh lab column of the chart. Your class answers may vary from the responses shown here, especially in the last row. Students can use extra paper to report more than one question.

Experiment / Elements	Eyelets	Searching the Forest	Distance vs. Time	Spreading Out	A Day at the Races	Flipping Two Coins	Soap Bubbles	Mass vs. Volume	Circumference vs. Diameter
Main Variables	number of eyelets, number of pairs of shoes	color, number of tiles pulled	distance and time	number of drops, area of spot	time, distance, speed	number of heads, percent of sample	length of time bubble "lives," percent of bubbles	volume of an object, mass of an object	diameter of a circle, circumference of a circle
Fixed Variables	definition of eyelets	sample size, rules for setting up bags, size of the tiles	pace, timing procedure	size of drop, type of towel, type of liquid, procedure for dropping liquid	timing procedure, distance in 6-yard race, time in 3-second race	procedure for flipping coins, same coins	type of bubble solution, room conditions, procedure for holding the bubble wand	type of material	procedure for measuring diameter and circumference
Variables Measured (units)	none	none	time in seconds, distance in yards	area in sq cm	time in seconds, distance in feet	none	time in seconds	mass in grams, volume in cc	length in cm, diameter in cm
Number of Trials	1	3	3	3	3	10, 100, 1000	Answers will vary.	1	1-diameter, 3-circumference
Type of Graph									
Important Questions (Answers may vary.)	How many eyelets on all the shoes in the class?	Predict the number of tiles of each color in the bag.	Find the speed that a person walks. How far can you walk in one hour?	Predict the area of a spot made with a different number of drops.	Compare speeds of students walking, running, etc.	Predict the percent of times heads will come up when flipping two coins many times.	Compare the shape of the graph to the shape of graphs which show the life spans of humans, American Robins, and oysters.	Does the relationship between mass and volume (density) depend on the material?	What is the relationship between the diameter of a circle and its circumference? Develop and use a formula for finding the circumference of a circle.

Figure 1: *A sample experiment review class chart*

After all groups report and the information is displayed, you can continue discussion using the following questions:

- *When doing an experiment, why do you need to keep some variables fixed?* (To be able to look for patterns and make predictions using the main variables in an experiment, you must hold other variables fixed. Students often think of this as "keeping the experiment fair." For example, to be able to make predictions about the distance a person can walk in a certain time, the person must keep his or her pace the same. In *Comparing Lives of Animals and Soap Bubbles,* students measured the life span of bubbles. To keep the experiment fair, it was necessary to keep the type of bubble solution the same.)

- *Why do we often have to do more than one trial when doing an experiment?* (One reason scientists use multiple trials is to check on large errors in measurement and in controlling fixed variables. Since error is often inevitable, scientists use multiple trials to average out the error. However, if large errors in measurement are not likely, one trial may suffice.)

- *How were point graphs used to make predictions?* (If the points lie close to a straight line, a line can be drawn which fits the points. This line is called the best-fit line. You can use this line to make predictions using interpolation or extrapolation.)

- *Name two experiments that are alike. How are they alike? How are they different?* (While answers may vary for this question, possible student responses follow. *Eyelets* and *Comparing Lives of Animals and Soap Bubbles* are alike because they both use bar graphs. In *Comparing Lives of Animals and Soap Bubbles,* you can use the shape of the graph to tell a story about the life spans of bubbles. *Mass vs. Volume* and *Circumference vs. Diameter* are alike because the graphs are straight lines through (0, 0). In *Mass vs. Volume,* the ratio of mass to volume $(\frac{M}{V})$ is density. In *Circumference vs. Diameter* the ratio of circumference to diameter $(\frac{C}{D})$ can be used to find the formula for the circumference of a circle.)

Journal Prompt

Which two experiments did you like the best? What did you like about each one? How are they alike? How are they different?

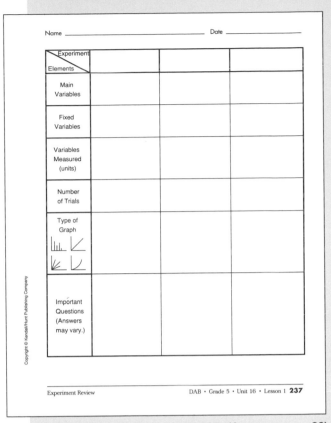

Discovery Assignment Book - page 237 (Answers on p. 32)

TIMS Tip

If students did not complete all the labs during the school year, you can adjust the chart as needed.

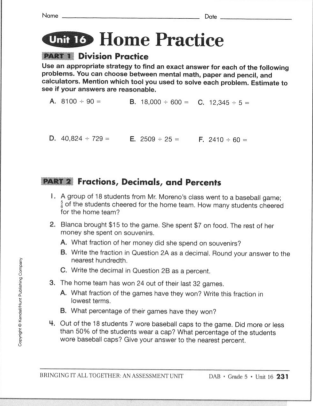

Discovery Assignment Book - page 231 *(Answers on p. 31)*

Homework and Practice

- Assign DPP Task B, which reviews computation, and DPP Challenge D, which reviews factors. You can also assign Bits A and C, which review fractions, percents, and circle graphs.

- Assign Part 1 of the Home Practice, which practices mental math and computation.

Answers for Part 1 of the Home Practice are in the Answer Key at the end of this lesson and at the end of this unit.

At a Glance

Math Facts and Daily Practice and Problems

Assign DPP items A–D. Item A reviews fractions in the context of a recipe. Task B practices computation. Item C reviews percents and circle graphs. Challenge D reviews factors.

Teaching the Activity

1. Read the opening paragraph of the *Experiment Review* Activity Page in the *Student Guide*.
2. Review the lab *Comparing Lives of Animals and Soap Bubbles* using **Question 2** in the *Student Guide* and the *Experiment Review Chart* Activity Pages in the *Discovery Assignment Book*.
3. Students work in groups to review other labs completed throughout the year using their portfolios and **Question 2.** Assign each group one (or two) labs to review.
4. Each group reports to the class on the labs they reviewed. The class creates a table showing the components of each lab.
5. Use the discussion prompts in the Lesson Guide to help students compare and contrast labs.

Homework

Assign Part 1 of the Home Practice.

Answer Key is on pages 31–32.

Notes:

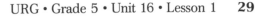

Comparing Lives of Animals and Soap Bubbles Lab

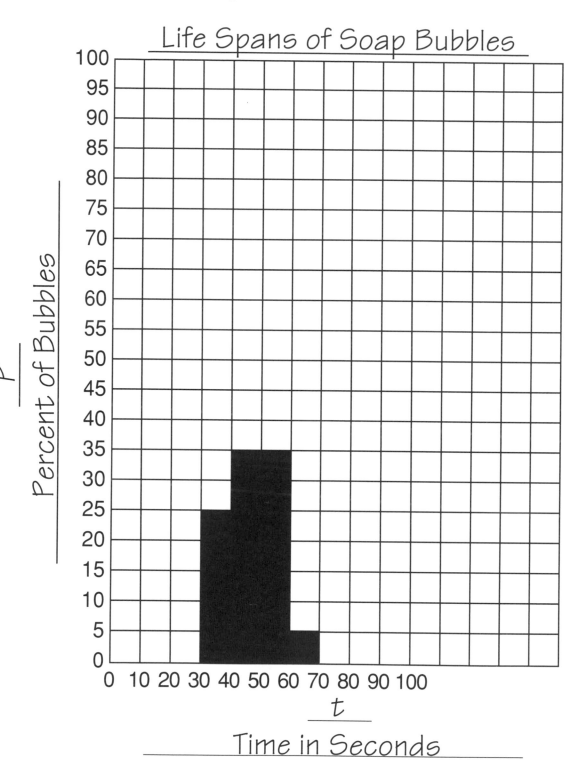

Life Spans of Soap Bubbles

Percent of Bubbles

$\dfrac{P}{}$

Time in Seconds

t

Transparency Master

Student Guide (p. 488)

Experiment Review

1. *Comparing Lives of Animals and Soap Bubbles*

2. **A.** Time at which bubble pops and percent of bubbles

   B. Yes. Type of bubble solution, room conditions, and procedure for holding the bubble wand.

   C. Time measured in seconds

   D. 1

   E. It was a bar graph with Time on the horizontal axis and Percent of Bubbles on the vertical axis.

   F. Comparing the shape of the Life Spans of Soap Bubbles graph with graphs that show the life spans of humans, American Robins, and oysters.

3. See Figure 1 in Lesson Guide 1 for a sample chart.*

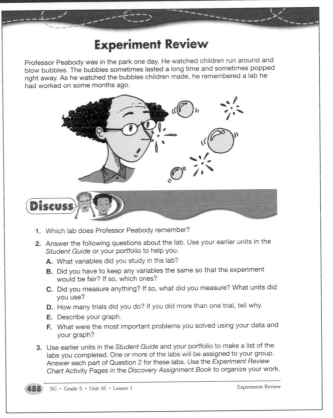

Experiment Review

Professor Peabody was in the park one day. He watched children run around and blow bubbles. The bubbles sometimes lasted a long time and sometimes popped right away. As he watched the bubbles children made, he remembered a lab he had worked on some months ago.

Discuss

1. Which lab does Professor Peabody remember?
2. Answer the following questions about the lab. Use your earlier units in the *Student Guide* or your portfolio to help you.
   A. What variables did you study in the lab?
   B. Did you have to keep any variables the same so that the experiment would be fair? If so, which ones?
   C. Did you measure anything? If so, what did you measure? What units did you use?
   D. How many trials did you do? If you did more than one trial, tell why.
   E. Describe your graph.
   F. What were the most important problems you solved using your data and your graph?
3. Use earlier units in the *Student Guide* and your portfolio to make a list of the labs you completed. One or more of the labs will be assigned to your group. Answer each part of Question 2 for these labs. Use the *Experiment Review Chart* Activity Pages in the *Discovery Assignment Book* to organize your work.

488   SG • Grade 5 • Unit 16 • Lesson 1   Experiment Review

Student Guide - page 488

Discovery Assignment Book (p. 231)

Home Practice†

Part 1. Division Practice

Choice of tools may vary.

  A. 90; mental math is an appropriate tool

  B. 30; mental math is an appropriate tool

  C. 2469; paper and pencil are appropriate tools

  D. 56; calculators are appropriate tools

  E. $100\frac{9}{25}$ or 100 R9; mental math or paper and pencil are appropriate tools

  F. $40\frac{1}{6}$ or 40 R10; mental math, paper and pencil, or calculators are appropriate tools

Name _____ Date _____

Unit 16 Home Practice

PART 1 Division Practice

Use an appropriate strategy to find an exact answer for each of the following problems. You can choose between mental math, paper and pencil, and calculators. Mention which tool you used to solve each problem. Estimate to see if your answers are reasonable.

  A. 8100 ÷ 90 =   B. 18,000 ÷ 600 =   C. 12,345 ÷ 5 =

  D. 40,824 ÷ 729 =   E. 2509 ÷ 25 =   F. 2410 ÷ 60 =

PART 2 Fractions, Decimals, and Percents

1. A group of 18 students from Mr. Moreno's class went to a baseball game; $\frac{5}{6}$ of the students cheered for the home team. How many students cheered for the home team?

2. Blanca brought $15 to the game. She spent $7 on food. The rest of her money she spent on souvenirs.
   A. What fraction of her money did she spend on souvenirs?
   B. Write the fraction in Question 2A as a decimal. Round your answer to the nearest hundredth.
   C. Write the decimal in Question 2B as a percent.

3. The home team has won 24 out of their last 32 games.
   A. What fraction of the games have they won? Write this fraction in lowest terms.
   B. What percentage of their games have they won?

4. Out of the 18 students 7 wore baseball caps to the game. Did more or less than 50% of the students wear a cap? What percentage of the students wore baseball caps? Give your answer to the nearest percent.

BRINGING IT ALL TOGETHER: AN ASSESSMENT UNIT   DAB • Grade 5 • Unit 16 **231**

Discovery Assignment Book - page 231

*Answers and/or discussion are included in the Lesson Guide.
†Answers for all the Home Practice in the *Discovery Assignment Book* are at the end of the unit.

Discovery Assignment Book (pp. 235–237)

Experiment Review Chart

See Figure 1 in Lesson Guide 1 for a complete table.

Name _____ Date _____

Experiment Review Chart

Experiment Elements			
Main Variables			
Fixed Variables			
Variables Measured (units)			
Number of Trials			
Type of Graph			
Important Questions (Answers may vary.)			

Copyright © Kendall/Hunt Publishing Company

Experiment Review   DAB • Grade 5 • Unit 16 • Lesson 1 **235**

Discovery Assignment Book - page 235

Name _____ Date _____

Experiment Elements			
Main Variables			
Fixed Variables			
Variables Measured (units)			
Number of Trials			
Type of Graph			
Important Questions (Answers may vary.)			

Copyright © Kendall/Hunt Publishing Company

236 DAB • Grade 5 • Unit 16 • Lesson 1   Experiment Review

Discovery Assignment Book - page 236

Name _____ Date _____

Experiment Elements			
Main Variables			
Fixed Variables			
Variables Measured (units)			
Number of Trials			
Type of Graph			
Important Questions (Answers may vary.)			

Copyright © Kendall/Hunt Publishing Company

Experiment Review   DAB • Grade 5 • Unit 16 • Lesson 1 **237**

Discovery Assignment Book - page 237

Lesson 2

Bats!

Lesson Overview

The story begins as Professor John Eagle and his children, Bobby and Sarah, hike up Frijoles Canyon located in Bandelier National Monument in New Mexico. They see archaeological sites on their way to their destination, a bat cave. The children meet an expert on bats and learn about the use of sampling to estimate populations of animals.

This *Adventure Book* story and the activity in Lesson 3 *More Bats!* provide the context for the assessment lab *How Many Bats in a Cave?* Students model the capture-recapture technique portrayed in the story to estimate the number of beans in a bag.

Key Content

- Sampling a population.
- Making predictions from samples.
- Using ratios and proportions to solve problems.
- Using numerical variables.
- Connecting mathematics and science to real-world situations.

Key Vocabulary

- Anasazi
- proportional
- pueblo
- ratio
- ruins
- tagged
- talus village

Math Facts

DPP item E provides practice with division facts.

Homework

1. Assign DPP Challenge F, which explores mass, volume, and density.
2. Assign Part 2 of the Home Practice, which reviews fractions, decimals, and percents.

Materials List

Supplies and Copies

Student	Teacher
Supplies for Each Student	**Supplies** • map of the United States, optional
Copies	**Copies/Transparencies**

All blackline masters including assessment, transparency, and DPP masters are also on the Teacher Resource CD.

Student Books
Bats! (*Adventure Book* Pages 93–106)

Daily Practice and Problems and Home Practice
DPP items E–F (*Unit Resource Guide* Page 14)
Home Practice Part 2 (*Discovery Assignment Book* Page 231)

Note: Classrooms whose pacing differs significantly from the suggested pacing of the units should use the Math Facts Calendar in Section 4 of the *Facts Resource Guide* to ensure students receive the complete math facts program.

Daily Practice and Problems

Suggestions for using the DPPs are on page 41.

E. Bit: Division Fact Practice (URG p. 14)

$\boxed{\begin{array}{c} 5 \\ \times 7 \end{array}}$

A. $50 \div 5 =$ B. $12 \div 3 =$

C. $90 \div 10 =$ D. $8 \div 2 =$

E. $24 \div 8 =$ F. $28 \div 7 =$

G. $56 \div 8 =$ H. $80 \div 8 =$

I. $4 \div 2 =$ J. $48 \div 8 =$

F. Challenge: Different Densities
(URG p. 14)

Lee Yah and Frank found the mass of 30 cc of vegetable oil and 30 cc of corn syrup. They found that the mass of the vegetable oil is 27 grams and the mass of the corn syrup is 41 grams.

1. Which is denser, vegetable oil or corn syrup? How do you know?

2. Predict what will happen if vegetable oil, water, and corn syrup are poured into the same container. Which liquid will float to the top? Which will sink to the bottom? Draw a picture showing the 3 liquids in the container.

3. Frank finds the mass of a plastic sphere to be 10 g and the volume to be 8.5 cc.

   A. If the sphere is placed in corn syrup, will it sink or float?

   B. If the sphere is placed in vegetable oil, will it sink or float?

Adventure Book - page 94

Ask students to read through the *Adventure Book* once before you discuss it so they can enjoy the story and get an overview of the ideas presented. Then use the following prompts to help you lead a class discussion:

Page 94

• *Locate Bandelier National Monument on a map.*

Bandelier National Monument is located on the Pajarito Plateau, west of Santa Fe, New Mexico. Bandelier was established in 1916 and covers nearly 50 square miles. Ninety percent of Bandelier National Monument is virtually undisturbed wild land, accessible by more than 70 miles of trails. Frijoles Canyon is the site of the Anasazi ruins and is of great archaeological value.

Translated, Frijoles Canyon means bean canyon. The cliff dwellers were farmers and grew corn, beans, and squash. The cliff ruins, or talus villages, extend along the canyon for approximately 2 miles. The masonry houses were from one to three stories high and had many cave rooms gouged out of the solid cliff. Many of the ruins have been dated back to the twelfth century. The following vocabulary will help students understand the story better:

talus village—cliff dwellings

Anasazi—Navajo for "the ancient ones"

pueblo—town

Page 97

- *How will Joan and the Eagle family catch a sample of the bats that live in the cave?*

They will use a trap to catch a sample of 100 to 150 bats as they fly out of the cave.

Adventure Book - page 97

Page 98

- *What does it mean to "tag" a bat?*

A small band with identifying information is placed on the bat's wrists. You can see an example on page 102.

- *How many bats has Joan tagged over the summer?*

1000 bats

- *When have we used sampling to make predictions?*

In Unit 1 Populations and Samples: *Eyelets* and *Searching the Forest.*

Adventure Book - page 98

Adventure Book - page 99

Page 99

- *Describe what is happening on page 99.*

It is dusk. The bats are leaving the cave to find food. Joan and the Eagle family have set up a trap to capture a sample of the bats that inhabit the cave.

Adventure Book - page 100

Page 100

- *How many bats were caught in the trap?*

About 100.

- *What data is Sarah recording?*

Sarah is recording the total number of bats and the number of bats that have tags. She is also recording whether the bats are male or female.

Page 102

Interesting related facts:

Bats are not blind. Actually in low-light situations such as dusk and dawn, most bats can see much better than humans. Their use of sonar called echolocation allows them to discern objects as tiny as a flying gnat in pitch darkness. Fishing bats have echolocation so sophisticated that they can detect a minnow's fin protruding only 2 millimeters above a pond's surface.

- *Exactly how many bats were in the sample? How many had tags?*

There were 105 bats in the sample. Nine had tags.

Adventure Book - page 102

Page 103

- *Joan has collected data before. What is the average number of tagged bats in a sample of 100 bats?*

She averages 10 tagged bats out of every 100 bats counted.

- *Write this as a ratio of tagged bats to total number of bats in a sample.*

$$\frac{10 \text{ tagged bats}}{100 \text{ bats in sample}}$$

- *Is this ratio close to $\frac{9 \text{ tagged bats}}{105 \text{ bats}}$? Why or why not?*

Yes. Since 9 is close to 10 and 105 is close to 100, $\frac{9}{105}$ is close to $\frac{10 \text{ tagged bats}}{100 \text{ bats}}$.

- *What is a similar way to write the ratio $\frac{10 \text{ tagged bats}}{100 \text{ bats}}$? (Hint: Reduce the fraction to lowest terms.)*

$$\frac{1 \text{ tagged bat}}{10 \text{ bats}}$$

- *Say this new ratio in words.*

The ratio of tagged bats to bats in the sample is about 1 to 10.

- *About what percent of the bats are tagged? (What is $\frac{1}{10}$ as a percent?)*

10%

Adventure Book - page 103

Adventure Book - page 104

Page 104

- *What variables are represented by t and T?*

Lower case *t* represents the number of tagged bats in the sample.

Capital *T* represents the number of tagged bats in the cave.

- *What variables are represented by n and N?*

Lower case *n* represents the number of bats in the sample.

Capital *N* represents the number of bats in the cave.

- *What are some equivalent fractions for $\frac{10}{100}$?*

$\frac{1}{10}$, $\frac{100}{1000}$, $\frac{1000}{10,000}$

Adventure Book - page 105

Page 105

- *Sarah wrote this proportion: $\frac{1}{10} = \frac{1000}{N}$. Why did Sarah use the ratio $\frac{1}{10}$?*

The fraction $\frac{1}{10}$ is the ratio of tagged bats in the sample to the total number of bats in the sample $\left(\frac{t}{n}\right)$. This is equal to the ratio of tagged bats in the cave to the total number of bats in the cave $\left(\frac{T}{N}\right)$.

- *Why did Sarah write 1000 for T?*

T is the number of tagged bats that live in the cave.

- *What does N stand for? What do Sarah and Bobby want to find out?*

N is the number of bats in the cave.

- *How did Sarah and Bobby decide that there were 10,000 bats in the cave?*

They used equivalent fractions to solve the proportion:

$$\frac{1}{10} = \frac{1000}{N}$$

$$\frac{1}{10} = \frac{1 \times 1000}{10 \times 1000} = \frac{1000}{10,000}$$

So, $N = 10,000$ bats. There are about 10,000 bats in the cave.

DPP item E practices division facts.

- Assign DPP Challenge F, which explores mass, volume, and density.

- Assign Part 2 of the Home Practice, which reviews fractions, decimals, and percents.

Answers for Part 2 of the Home Practice are in the Answer Key at the end of this lesson and at the end of this unit.

- Bandelier National Monument World Wide Web site (http://www.nps.gov/band/).

- Barbour and Davis. *Bats of America.* Books on Demand, Ann Arbor, MI, 1994.

- Bat Conservation International World Wide Web site (http://www.batcon.org/).

Name _____ Date _____

Unit 16 Home Practice

PART 1 Division Practice

Use an appropriate strategy to find an exact answer for each of the following problems. You can choose between mental math, paper and pencil, and calculators. Mention which tool you used to solve each problem. Estimate to see if your answers are reasonable.

A. $8100 \div 90 =$ B. $18,000 \div 600 =$ C. $12,345 \div 5 =$

D. $40,824 \div 729 =$ E. $2509 \div 25 =$ F. $2410 \div 60 =$

PART 2 Fractions, Decimals, and Percents

1. A group of 18 students from Mr. Moreno's class went to a baseball game; $\frac{2}{3}$ of the students cheered for the home team. How many students cheered for the home team?

2. Blanca brought $15 to the game. She spent $7 on food. The rest of her money she spent on souvenirs.
   A. What fraction of her money did she spend on souvenirs?
   B. Write the fraction in Question 2A as a decimal. Round your answer to the nearest hundredth.
   C. Write the decimal in Question 2B as a percent.

3. The home team has won 24 out of their last 32 games.
   A. What fraction of the games have they won? Write this fraction in lowest terms.
   B. What percentage of their games have they won?

4. Out of the 18 students 7 wore baseball caps to the game. Did more or less than 50% of the students wear a cap? What percentage of the students wore baseball caps? Give your answer to the nearest percent.

BRINGING IT ALL TOGETHER: AN ASSESSMENT UNIT   DAB • Grade 5 • Unit 16 **231**

Discovery Assignment Book **- page 231** *(Answers on p. 42)*

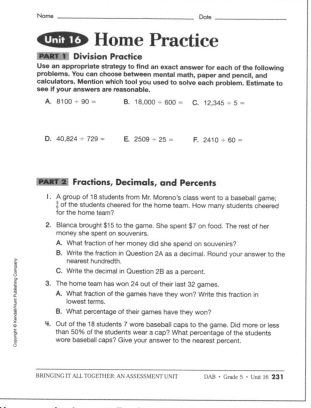

Discovery Assignment Book - page 231

Discovery Assignment Book (p. 231)

Home Practice*

Part 2. Fractions, Decimals, and Percents

1. 15 students

2. A. $\frac{8}{15}$ B. 0.53   C. 53%

3. A. $\frac{24}{32} = \frac{3}{4}$ B. 75%

4. Less than 50%; 39% of the students wore baseball caps.

*Answers for all the Home Practice in the *Discovery Assignment Book* are at the end of the unit.

Lesson 3

More Bats!

Lesson Overview

Estimated Class Sessions

1

This lesson continues the story of John Eagle, Bobby, and Sarah as they collect data on the number of tagged bats in each capture. They are investigating whether the number of tagged bats in a sample *(t)* is really proportional to the total number of bats in a sample *(n)*. Students graph the data presented in the *Student Guide*. They use their best-fit lines to find the ratio of the number of tagged bats in a sample to the total number of bats in a sample $(\frac{t}{n})$.

This lesson is a prerequisite for the assessment lab in Lesson 4. It reviews using best-fit lines to solve proportional reasoning problems.

Key Content

- Drawing and interpreting best-fit lines.
- Writing ratios as fractions.
- Finding equal ratios.
- Using words, tables, graphs, and fractions to express ratios.
- Using numerical variables.
- Translating between different representations of ratios (graphical and symbolic).

Math Facts

Complete DPP item G, which reviews the division facts.

Assessment

Use the *Observational Assessment Record* to note students' abilities to express ratios using words, tables, graphs, and fractions.

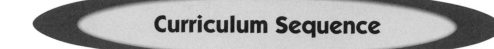

Curriculum Sequence

Before This Unit

Students investigated the connections between ratios, proportions, and graphing in Unit 13. They used graphs to help solve proportional reasoning problems in labs and activities in Units 3, 4, 5, 13, and 14.

Materials List

Supplies and Copies

Student	Teacher
Supplies for Each Student • calculator • ruler	**Supplies**
Copies • 1 copy of *Centimeter Graph Paper* per student (*Unit Resource Guide* Page 49)	**Copies/Transparencies** • 1 copy of *Observational Assessment Record* to be used throughtout this unit (*Unit Resource Guide* Pages 9–10)

All blackline masters including assessment, transparency, and DPP masters are also on the Teacher Resource CD.

Student Books
More Bats! (*Student Guide* Pages 489–491)
Bats! (*Adventure Book* Pages 93–106)

Daily Practice and Problems and Home Practice
DPP items G–H (*Unit Resource Guide* Page 15)

Note: Classrooms whose pacing differs significantly from the suggested pacing of the units should use the Math Facts Calendar in Section 4 of the *Facts Resource Guide* to ensure students receive the complete math facts program.

Assessment Tools
Observational Assessment Record (*Unit Resource Guide* Pages 9–10)

Daily Practice and Problems

Suggestions for using the DPPs are on page 48.

G. Bit: Division Fact Practice (URG p. 15)

A. $40 \div 10 = n$

B. $n \div 5 = 4$

C. $49 \div n = 7$

D. $27 \div n = 3$

E. $72 \div n = 9$

F. $21 \div 3 = n$

G. $n \div 8 = 2$

H. $n \div 5 = 8$

I. $100 \div 10 = n$

J. $9 \div 3 = n$

K. $n \div 2 = 5$

L. $42 \div n = 7$

H. Challenge: The Box Collection
(URG p. 15)

Irma has four new boxes to add to her box collection, which she displays at home in the living room. She places a piece of felt beneath each box so it does not scratch her mother's coffee table. She begins with a rectangular piece of felt that measures 8 inches by 16 inches. She cuts a square off each corner of the felt. She needs two squares that are 4 inches on a side, a square that is 3 inches on a side, and a square that is 2 inches on a side.

1. How much felt will she have left?
2. Draw the piece of felt on a piece of *Centimeter Grid Paper.* Show the squares Irma is cutting out. Find the perimeter of the remaining piece of felt.

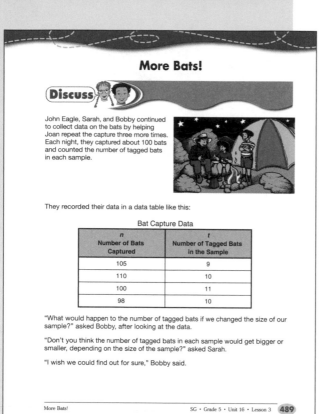

More Bats!

Discuss

John Eagle, Sarah, and Bobby continued to collect data on the bats by helping Joan repeat the capture three more times. Each night, they captured about 100 bats and counted the number of tagged bats in each sample.

They recorded their data in a data table like this:

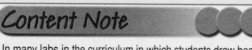

Bat Capture Data

n Number of Bats Captured	t Number of Tagged Bats in the Sample
105	9
110	10
100	11
98	10

"What would happen to the number of tagged bats if we changed the size of our sample?" asked Bobby, after looking at the data.

"Don't you think the number of tagged bats in each sample would get bigger or smaller, depending on the size of the sample?" asked Sarah.

"I wish we could find out for sure," Bobby said.

More Bats!   SG • Grade 5 • Unit 16 • Lesson 3   **489**

Student Guide - page 489

Content Note

In many labs in the curriculum in which students draw best-fit lines, three values for the responding variable are averaged and the average value is plotted. This averages out experimental or measurement error.

In this lab, a different method is used. The conservation club recaptured the bats four times for each sample size and recorded both the total number of bats in each recapture and the number of tagged bats in each recapture. This resulted in 12 entries in the data table. Instead of recording averages in the data table, we plot all 12 points and use the best-fit line to "average" out the experimental error. Plotting all the data points—instead of averaging the data before plotting points—results in a graph with more information since it also shows the spread of the data.

Review the Adventure Book *Bats!* with students before beginning this activity.

Teaching the Activity

Begin by asking students to read the vignette on the *More Bats!* Activity Pages in the *Student Guide*. *Question 1* asks students to make a graph of all the data collected by the conservation club. They plot the number of bats captured *(n)* on the horizontal axis and the number of tagged bats in the sample *(t)* on the vertical axis. They then add the data collected by John Eagle, Sarah, and Bobby to their graphs in *Question 2.* Students will see that the points form three distinct clusters or groupings on their graph *(Question 3A).*

They add the point ($n = 0$, $t = 0$) to their graph since there will be no tagged bats when there are no bats in a sample *(Question 3B).* A best-fit line is then drawn through the points *(Question 3C).* Remind students that when drawing their best-fit lines, they should try to draw the lines so there are about as many points above the line as below the line. A sample graph is shown in Figure 2.

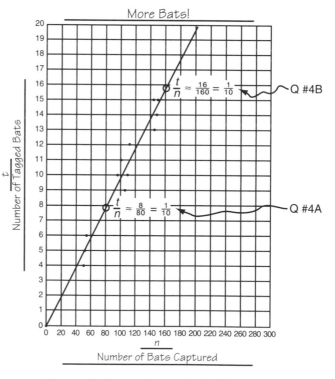

Figure 2: *A sample graph for* More Bats!

Question 4 asks students to write two ratios using the best-fit line. Figure 2 shows these ratios. For our best-fit line, when $n = 80$, t is about 7.8 and when $n = 160$, t is about 15.7. For the purpose of this activity, it is sufficient to round the values of t to the nearest whole number. So, for $n = 80$, we get $t = 8$ and for $n = 160$, we get $t = 16$. The two ratios of n to t are equivalent.

$$\frac{8}{80} = \frac{16}{160} = \frac{1}{10}$$

The ratio $\frac{1}{10}$ matches the ratio Joan reported in the *Adventure Book* and is approximately equal to the ratio of tagged bats to bats in the sample that John Eagle, Bobby, and Sarah found after their first capture. *Question 5* asks students to choose other points from the line and write ratios corresponding to those points. They can see that all the ratios $\frac{t}{n}$ are equal (or approximately equal). Therefore, we can use the ratio of tagged bats in the sample to the total number of bats in the sample $\frac{t}{n}$ to estimate the number of bats in the total population.

Question 6 poses the same question asked by Bobby and Sarah in the vignette at the beginning of the lesson. What happens to the number of tagged bats in a sample as the sample size changes? The number of tagged bats increases if the sample size increases and decreases if the sample size decreases. In particular, the number of tagged bats changes in proportion to the number of bats in a sample.

Question 7 asks students to explain how Sarah and Bobby can use the data collected by the conservation club to support their estimate of 10,000 bats in the cave. The Eagle children used the ratio $\frac{t}{n} = \frac{1 \text{ tagged bat}}{10 \text{ bats}}$ captured to calculate their estimate. Since the ratio of tagged bats to bats captured remains approximately $\frac{1}{10}$ no matter the size of the sample, the new data support their estimate.

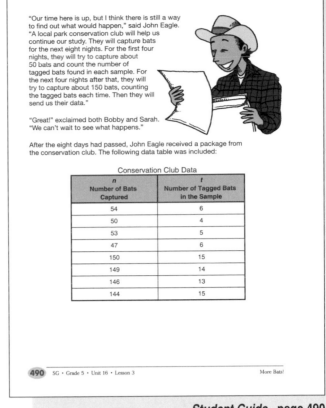

"Our time here is up, but I think there is still a way to find out what would happen," said John Eagle. "A local park conservation club will help us continue our study. They will capture bats for the next eight nights. For the first four nights, they will try to capture about 50 bats and count the number of tagged bats found in each sample. For the next four nights after that, they will try to capture about 150 bats, counting the tagged bats each time. Then they will send us their data."

"Great!" exclaimed both Bobby and Sarah. "We can't wait to see what happens."

After the eight days had passed, John Eagle received a package from the conservation club. The following data table was included:

Conservation Club Data

n Number of Bats Captured	t Number of Tagged Bats in the Sample
54	6
50	4
53	5
47	6
150	15
149	14
146	13
144	15

Student Guide - page 490

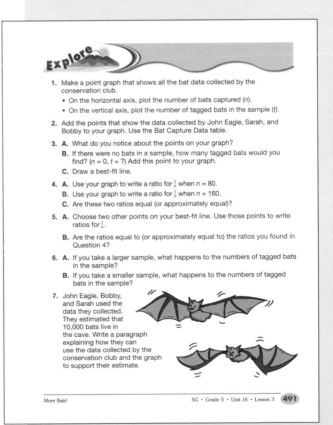

Explore

1. Make a point graph that shows all the bat data collected by the conservation club.
   • On the horizontal axis, plot the number of bats captured (*n*).
   • On the vertical axis, plot the number of tagged bats in the sample (*t*).
2. Add the points that show the data collected by John Eagle, Sarah, and Bobby to your graph. Use the Bat Capture Data table.
3. A. What do you notice about the points on your graph?
   B. If there were no bats in a sample, how many tagged bats would you find? ($n = 0$, $t = ?$) Add this point to your graph.
   C. Draw a best-fit line.
4. A. Use your graph to write a ratio for $\frac{t}{n}$ when $n = 80$.
   B. Use your graph to write a ratio for $\frac{t}{n}$ when $n = 160$.
   C. Are these two ratios equal (or approximately equal)?
5. A. Choose two other points on your best-fit line. Use those points to write ratios for $\frac{t}{n}$.
   B. Are the ratios equal to (or approximately equal to) the ratios you found in Question 4?
6. A. If you take a larger sample, what happens to the numbers of tagged bats in the sample?
   B. If you take a smaller sample, what happens to the numbers of tagged bats in the sample?
7. John Eagle, Bobby, and Sarah used the data they collected. They estimated that 10,000 bats live in the cave. Write a paragraph explaining how they can use the data collected by the conservation club and the graph to support their estimate.

Student Guide - page 491 (Answers on p. 50)

Math Facts

Assign DPP item G, which uses variables to practice the division facts.

Homework and Practice

Assign DPP item H, which is a challenging problem about area and perimeter.

Assessment

Use the *Observational Assessment Record* to note students' abilities to express ratios using words, tables, graphs, and fractions.

Estimated Class Sessions

1

At a Glance

Math Facts and Daily Practice and Problems

Complete DPP items G–H. DPP item G reviews the division facts while DPP Challenge H reviews area and perimeter.

Teaching the Activity

1. Review the Adventure Book *Bats!*
2. Read the vignette on the *More Bats!* Activity Pages in the *Student Guide*.
3. Students make a point graph displaying all the data collected by the conservation club. *(Question 1)*
4. Students add the points collected by John Eagle, Bobby, and Sarah and draw a best-fit line. *(Questions 2–3)*
5. Students use the best-fit line to write the ratio $\frac{t}{n}$ and to decide if the variables t and n are in proportion. *(Questions 4–5)*
6. Students use the graph to analyze the new data. *(Questions 6–7)*

Assessment

Use the *Observational Assessment Record* to note students' abilities to express ratios using words, tables, graphs, and fractions.

Answer Key is on page 50.

Notes:

Name _____ Date _____

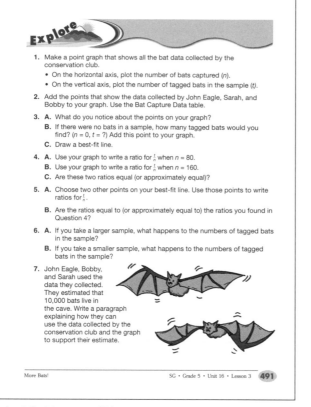

Explore

1. Make a point graph that shows all the bat data collected by the conservation club.
   - On the horizontal axis, plot the number of bats captured (*n*).
   - On the vertical axis, plot the number of tagged bats in the sample (*t*).

2. Add the points that show the data collected by John Eagle, Sarah, and Bobby to your graph. Use the Bat Capture Data table.

3. A. What do you notice about the points on your graph?
   B. If there were no bats in a sample, how many tagged bats would you find? (*n* = 0, *t* = ?) Add this point to your graph.
   C. Draw a best-fit line.

4. A. Use your graph to write a ratio for $\frac{t}{n}$ when *n* = 80.
   B. Use your graph to write a ratio for $\frac{t}{n}$ when *n* = 160.
   C. Are these two ratios equal (or approximately equal)?

5. A. Choose two other points on your best-fit line. Use those points to write ratios for $\frac{t}{n}$.
   B. Are the ratios equal to (or approximately equal to) the ratios you found in Question 4?

6. A. If you take a larger sample, what happens to the numbers of tagged bats in the sample?
   B. If you take a smaller sample, what happens to the numbers of tagged bats in the sample?

7. John Eagle, Bobby, and Sarah used the data they collected. They estimated that 10,000 bats live in the cave. Write a paragraph explaining how they can use the data collected by the conservation club and the graph to support their estimate.

More Bats!   SG • Grade 5 • Unit 16 • Lesson 3   **491**

Student Guide - page 491

Student Guide (p. 491)

1.–2.* See Figure 2 in Lesson Guide 3.

3.* A. The points form three distinct clusters or groupings on the graph.

     B. If there are no bats in the sample, there will be no tagged bats. (*n* = 0, *t* = 0)

     C. See Figure 2 in the Lesson Guide.

4.* A. $\frac{t}{n} = \frac{8}{80}$ B. $\frac{t}{n} = \frac{16}{160}$

     C. Yes, since these two ratios can be reduced to $\frac{1}{10}$, they are equivalent.

5. A. Ratios will vary, however, all ratios should be approximately equal to $\frac{1}{10}$.*

     B. Yes

6.* A.–B. As the sample size gets larger, the number of tagged bats gets larger. As the sample size gets smaller, the number of tagged bats gets smaller.

7. See Lesson Guide 3.*

---

*Answers and/or discussion are included in the Lesson Guide.

Lesson 4
How Many Bats in a Cave?

Lesson Overview

Estimated Class Sessions
3

Using beans in a container to represent bats in a cave, students simulate the capture-recapture technique described in the Adventure Book *Bats!* Using this technique, graphing, and proportional reasoning, students can get an approximation of the total number of "bats" in their "cave."

Key Content

- Collecting, organizing, graphing, and analyzing data.
- Drawing and interpreting best-fit lines.
- Making predictions from samples.
- Using patterns in tables and graphs to solve problems.
- Using ratios and proportions to solve problems.
- Translating between different representations of ratios (graphical and symbolic).
- Using numerical variables.
- Translating between graphs and real-world events.
- Connecting mathematics and science to real-world situations.
- Using the Student Rubric: *Telling* to self-assess communication skills.

Key Vocabulary

- capture-recapture
- sampling

Math Facts

Assign DPP item I, which reviews the division facts.

Homework

1. Assign the homework in the *Student Guide*. Students will need a piece of *Centimeter Graph Paper*.
2. Assign Parts 3 and 4 of the Home Practice.

Assessment

Choose one or more sections of the lab to use as an assessment.

Materials List

Supplies and Copies

Student	Teacher
Supplies for Each Student • ruler • calculator **Supplies for Each Student Group** • brightly colored markers for tagging the beans • self-closing bag filled with 1 lb. of baby lima beans • 3 sizes of scoops: small (about 2 tablespoons), medium (about 4 tablespoons), and large (about 6 tablespoons)	**Supplies**
Copies • 1 copy of *Three-column Data Table* per student, optional (*Unit Resource Guide* Page 63) • 2 copies of *Centimeter Graph Paper* per student (*Unit Resource Guide* Page 49)	**Copies/Transparencies** • 1 transparency of *Centimeter Graph Paper*, optional (*Unit Resource Guide* Page 49) • 1 copy of *TIMS Multidimensional Rubric*, optional (*Teacher Implementation Guide*, Assessment section)

All blackline masters including assessment, transparency, and DPP masters are also on the Teacher Resource CD.

Student Books

How Many Bats in a Cave? (*Student Guide* Pages 492–497)
Student Rubric: *Telling* (*Student Guide* Appendix C and Inside Back Cover), optional

Daily Practice and Problems and Home Practice

DPP items I–N (*Unit Resource Guide* Pages 16–18)
Home Practice Parts 3–4 (*Discovery Assignment Book* Page 232)

Note: Classrooms whose pacing differs significantly from the suggested pacing of the units should use the Math Facts Calendar in Section 4 of the *Facts Resource Guide* to ensure students receive the complete math facts program.

Assessment Tools

TIMS Multidimensional Rubric (*Teacher Implementation Guide*, Assessment section)

I. Bit: Division Fact Practice (URG p. 16) $\boxed{\frac{5}{\times 7}}$

A. $36 \div 6 =$

B. $180 \div 20 =$

C. $300 \div 50 =$

D. $3000 \div 100 =$

E. $160 \div 40 =$

F. $36,000 \div 400 =$

G. $450 \div 90 =$

H. $1200 \div 60 =$

I. $18,000 \div 600 =$

J. $81,000 \div 90 =$

K. $630 \div 90 =$

L. $60,000 \div 6 =$

J. Task: Practice (URG p. 16)

Solve the following using mental math or paper and pencil. Estimate to be sure your answers are reasonable.

A. $48 \times 28 =$ B. $280 \times 7 =$

C. $3006 \div 6 =$ D. $3.4 \times 0.14 =$

E. $7819 \div 46 =$ F. $57.83 + 213.77 =$

K. Bit: Finding Area (URG p. 17)

1. What is the area of a triangle whose base is 8 cm and height is 8 cm?
2. If the height is doubled, what is the area?
3. If the height is tripled, what is the area?

L. Task: In Proportion

(URG p. 17)

Solve the following. Explain your solutions.

1. If a hotel charges $270 for a 6-night stay, how much is a 2-night stay?
2. If I walk half a mile in ten minutes, how far can I walk in one hour?
3. For every eight children on a field trip there needs to be one adult chaperone. If there are 136 students going on the trip, how many chaperones are needed?
4. For every $20 the students collect in the school fundraiser, $5 goes toward decorating the cafeteria. If $1315 went toward the decoration project, how much money was collected in all?

M. Bit: Fractions (URG p. 17)

Use mental math or paper and pencil to solve the following.

A. $5\frac{7}{10} + 3\frac{1}{5} =$ B. $7\frac{4}{5} + 3\frac{1}{4} =$

C. $\frac{1}{2} - \frac{4}{9} =$ D. $1\frac{1}{2} + 2\frac{1}{4} =$

N. Challenge: Carnival (URG p. 18)

Admission to the carnival is $2. Then every ride costs 50 cents.

1. Manny and his two brothers together spent $24. They each rode the same number of rides. How many rides did each of the boys go on?
2. Lee Yah does not have to pay the admission fee since she is working a game booth. If she spends $4 on rides, how many rides did she go on?
3. Blanca started with $10. She spent some of her money on rides. She also tried her hand at a ring toss game. It costs $1 for 5 rings. Blanca tossed 15 rings. She now has $4.50 left.

   A. How many rides has Blanca already gone on?
   B. If she wants to buy popcorn for $0.75 and then go on more rides, how many more rides can she go on?

The sample data in the Lesson Guide was obtained by carrying out the experiment with one pound of baby lima beans. You can substitute other beans for the baby limas, but this can result in significantly different data. It is best for you to try out the activity beforehand to check that you get reasonable data, particularly if you use a different kind of bean.

Before the Lab

Use the Adventure Book *Bats!* in Lesson 2 to introduce the capture-recapture technique. Then students need to complete the activity *More Bats!* to review using best-fit lines to solve proportional reasoning problems.

Prepare a "bat cave" for each team of four students by placing 1 pound of baby lima beans in a self-closing plastic bag. Identify each bat cave with a different letter or name, such as Frijoles Cave or Lima Cave.

Examples of possible small, medium, and large scoops:

Small scoops: coffee scoop; $\frac{1}{8}$-c measuring cup, or a 1-oz portion cup

Medium scoops: $\frac{1}{4}$-c measuring cup or a 2-oz portion cup

Large scoops: $\frac{1}{3}$-c measuring cup or a 3-oz portion cup

You can use a $\frac{1}{2}$-c measuring cup, but the large number of beans will take a long time to count. Portion cups (1 oz, 2 oz, and 3 oz) can be found in restaurant supply sections of the market. Students may also use a tablespoon, scooping 2 tablespoons for the small sample, 4 tablespoons for the medium sample, and 6 tablespoons for the large sample.

Teaching the Lab

Part 1 Preparing for the Lab, Tagging the Bats, and Sampling the Bat Population

Discuss the use of sampling by asking students to recall the process in the lab *Searching the Forest*. In that lab, they used square-inch tiles in a bag to model a population of animals in a rain forest and estimated the population's makeup by investigating several samples of tiles in the bag. In this lab, we simulate a capture-recapture method to find an approximate number for the total number of bats in a cave. We model this process using beans in a bag to simulate bats in a cave.

The process is outlined on the *How Many Bats in a Cave?* Lab Pages in the *Student Guide.* Ask students to imagine that each bean is a bat and the bag is a bat cave. Students first tag 250 beans (bats) in their bags (caves).

After thoroughly mixing the tagged beans with the untagged beans, students take repeated samples of beans and count the number of tagged beans as well as the total number of beans in each sample. They find the ratio of tagged to total beans in the samples, then use equal ratios to estimate the total number of beans in the bag.

$$\frac{\text{number of tagged beans in a sample } (t)}{\text{total number of beans in a sample } (n)} =$$

$$\frac{\text{number of tagged beans in the bag } (T)}{\text{total number of beans in the bag } (N)}$$

$$\frac{t}{n} = \frac{250}{N}$$

The Tagging the Bats section of the *How Many Bats in a Cave?* Lab Pages in the *Student Guide* directs students to remove 250 beans from their bags, tag them by marking them on both sides with a brightly colored marker, and mix them with the rest of the beans. You may want to ask students to place paper on their desks while they color the beans, so they won't get marker on their desks. They can complete this step before they draw the picture.

TIMS Tip

Using spray paint to color the beans will speed up the tagging process. If you use smaller beans, you may need to tag more than 250 beans and use smaller scoops. If you use larger beans, you may need to tag fewer than 250 beans and use larger scoops.

After reading the Sampling the Bat Population section of the *Student Guide,* the class should develop a consistent sampling procedure using the scoops. All small samples should have approximately the same number of beans, all medium samples should have approximately the same number of beans, and so on. For clarity, model the scooping procedure for the class.

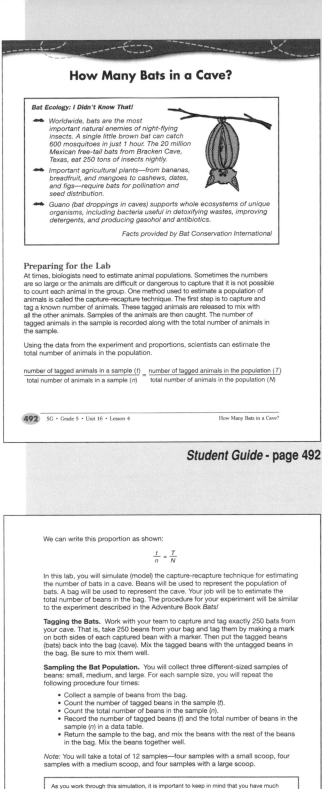

Student Guide - page 492

Student Guide - page 493

Figure 3: *A picture of the lab*

Part 2 Drawing the Picture

When students have a clear idea of what they are going to do, ask them to draw a picture showing the procedure and the key variables *(Question 1)*. A sample picture is shown in Figure 3.

The picture should include:

- The cave with tagged and untagged beans.
- A sample of beans indicating that the number of tagged beans and the total number of beans in each sample will be counted.
- The variables labeled with symbols (t and n).

Question 2 asks what variables the lab involves. The object of the lab is to use two equal ratios to estimate the total number of beans in the bag *(N),* so this is an important variable. To find this estimate, we need to find values for the total number of beans in each sample *(n),* the number of tagged beans in each sample *(t),* and the number of tagged beans in the bag *(T).* Since $T = 250$ for the whole experiment, it is a fixed variable and students know this value before they begin sampling *(Question 3A).* When we finish the experiment, we will be able to use the values in the data table to estimate a ratio for $\frac{t}{n}$ and use it to find the total number of beans in the bag *(N) (Question 3B).*

It is important to thoroughly mix the tagged and untagged beans so random samples of beans of the same sample size will have approximately the same number of tagged beans *(Question 4).*

Part 3 Collecting the Data

Students are asked to design their own data table and there are many ways to do this *(Question 5).* One way to organize the data into a table is shown in Figure 4. Students may use a *Three-column Data Table* to help them arrange the data. *Question 6* asks students to collect the data. They need to collect 12 pieces of data, four for each sample size, recording the total number of beans in the sample *(n)* and the number of tagged beans in the sample *(t).* It may also help to indicate whether the data are from the small, medium, or large scoop. Any table that allows them to retrieve the information easily should be acceptable.

> **TIMS Tip**
>
> If time is limited for collecting data, 3 samples can be taken for each size scoop. However, the more data collected, the more accurate the results will be.

Bat Cave Data

Sample Size	Total Number of Beans in Sample n	Number of Tagged Beans in Sample t
small	66	12
small	73	13
small	67	15
small	71	12
medium	122	26
medium	142	22
medium	129	29
medium	147	36
large	217	41
large	226	47
large	234	48
large	210	39

Figure 4: *Sample data for 1 oz, 2 oz, and 3 oz cups using baby lima beans*

Part 4 Graphing the Data

Students plot n on the horizontal axis and t on the vertical axis *(Question 7)*. Students should choose a scale for both axes that spreads out the data so accurate values of n and t can be read from the line. If there are no beans in the sample, there will be no tagged beans in the sample either, so students should add the point $(n = 0, t = 0)$ to the graph. They then draw a best-fit line. A graph of the sample data is shown in Figure 5.

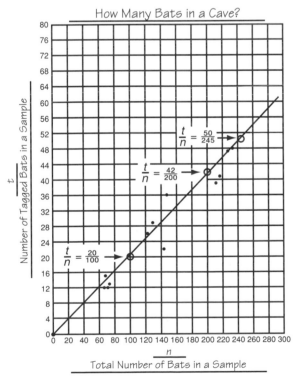

How Many Bats in a Cave?

$\frac{t}{n} = \frac{50}{245}$

$\frac{t}{n} = \frac{42}{200}$

$\frac{t}{n} = \frac{20}{100}$

t — Number of Tagged Bats in a Sample

n — Total Number of Bats in a Sample

Figure 5: *Graph of the sample data*

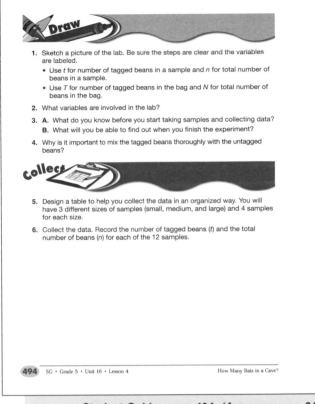

Student Guide - page 494 (Answers on p. 64)

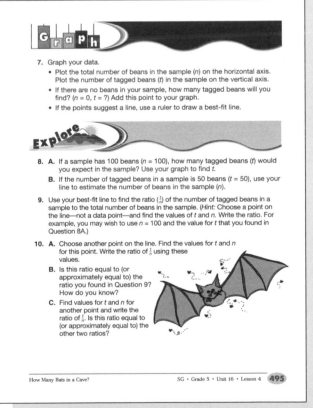

Student Guide - page 495 (Answers on p. 64)

TIMS Tip

If the ratios are not equivalent (or approximately equivalent), students may have made one or more errors in their graphs. The line must be a straight line through (0, 0) to use it to find equivalent ratios. Some students may need to redraw their lines more carefully with a ruler and be sure that they go through the center of all clusters of data points. Another common error is for students to read the graph incorrectly and choose an incorrect value for *t* or *n*. Errors in scaling the axes will also result in incorrect values for *t* or *n*.

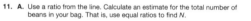

11. A. Use a ratio from the line. Calculate an estimate for the total number of beans in your bag. That is, use equal ratios to find *N*.

$$\frac{\text{number of tagged beans in a sample } (t)}{\text{total number of beans in a sample } (n)} = \frac{\text{number of tagged beans in the bag } (T)}{\text{total number of beans in the bag } (N)}$$

$$\frac{t}{n} = \frac{250}{N}$$

   B. Explain how you made your estimate. Use the Student Rubric: *Telling* as a guide.

12. Look at the data in your table.
   A. If you had only taken one sample, would the data give you a good estimate for the total number of beans in your bag? Why or why not?
   B. You took four samples for each sample size. Do you recommend the same, more, or fewer samples? Why?

Bat Trivia

- The world's smallest mammal is the bumblebee bat of Thailand, weighing less than a penny.
- Giant flying foxes that live in Indonesia have wingspans of nearly 6 feet.

Facts provided by Bat Conservation International

Student Guide - page 496 (Answers on p. 65)

Part 5 Exploring the Data

Question 8 asks students to use the graph to find a value for *t* that corresponds to $n = 100$ and a value for *n* when $t = 50$. The points for these values are circled on the sample graph in Figure 5 and can be used in *Question 9* to find the ratios of $\frac{t}{n}$:

$$\frac{t}{n} = \frac{20 \text{ tagged beans}}{100 \text{ beans in sample}}$$

$$\frac{t}{n} = \frac{50 \text{ tagged beans}}{245 \text{ beans in sample}}$$

If we choose another point on the line and use it to write a ratio for $\frac{t}{n}$, we can see that the ratios are equal or approximately equal *(Question 10).* For example, the value for *(t)* when $n = 200$ bats is about 42, so the ratio of $\frac{t}{n}$ is:

$$\frac{t}{n} = \frac{42 \text{ tagged beans}}{200 \text{ beans in sample}}$$

Using a calculator, we can find the decimal equivalent for each ratio rounded to the nearest hundredth: $\frac{20}{100} = 0.20$, $\frac{50}{245} = .20$, and $\frac{42}{200} = 0.21$. So, each of the three ratios taken from the line are approximately equal to one another. (See Figure 5.) If we look at these fractions, we see that they are each approximately equivalent to $\frac{1 \text{ tagged bean}}{5 \text{ beans}}$ or one tagged bean for every 5 beans in a sample.

Question 11 asks students to use the data they collected to estimate the total number of beans in their bag and to explain their solution strategies. There are many possible solution paths and answers will vary slightly. However, since all groups started with about 1 pound of beans, their estimates for the total number of beans *(N)* should be relatively close.

To solve the problem, we assume the following two ratios are equal to one another:

$$\frac{\text{number of tagged beans in a sample } (t)}{\text{total number of beans in a sample } (n)} =$$

$$\frac{\text{number of tagged beans in the bag } (250)}{\text{total number of beans in the bag } (N)}$$

Students choose a ratio from a point on the line and set up a proportion:

$$\frac{50 \text{ tagged beans}}{245 \text{ beans}} = \frac{250 \text{ tagged beans}}{N}$$

To find *N,* we can multiply numerator and denominator by the same number. Since 50×5 is 250, we can multiply numerator and denominator by 5 to find a fraction that is equal to $\frac{50}{245}$.

$$\frac{50 \text{ tagged beans}}{245 \text{ beans}} = \frac{50 \times 5}{245 \times 5} = \frac{250 \text{ tagged beans}}{N}$$

So, we estimate that there are about 245×5 or 1225 beans in the bag.

Another solution path uses the ratio 1 tagged bean out of every 5 beans in the sample:

$$\frac{1 \text{ tagged bean}}{5 \text{ beans}} = \frac{250 \text{ tagged beans}}{N}$$

$$\frac{1 \text{ tagged bean}}{5 \text{ beans}} = \frac{1 \times 250}{5 \times 250} = \frac{250 \text{ tagged beans}}{N}$$

Using this method, we estimate that $N = 5 \times 250$ or 1250 beans in the bag. Note that our two estimates are very close. Encourage students to solve the problem in more than one way to check their results, and to give clear and complete explanations of their methods.

Math Facts

DPP item I reviews the division facts using multiples of 10.

Homework and Practice

- Assign the Homework section in the *Student Guide* at the end of the lab. Students will need a piece of graph paper to complete the homework.

- Assign DPP items J, K, L, M, and N. DPP items J and M practice computation with whole numbers, decimals, and fractions. Bit K reviews finding the area of triangles. Task L reviews proportions. Challenge N involves problem solving with money.

- Assign Part 3 of the Home Practice to review fractions and mixed numbers and Part 4 to review circumference, perimeter, and area.

Answers for Parts 3 and 4 of the Home Practice are in the Answer Key at the end of this lesson and at the end of this unit.

Assessment

Grade one or more parts of the lab by assigning points to each section you choose to assess. Use the following criteria:

Drawing the Picture

- Does the picture include a bag of beans with some beans tagged and some untagged?
- Does it illustrate the sampling procedure?
- Are the variables (t, n) clearly labeled?

Collecting and Recording the Data

- Are the data organized in a table?
- Are the columns in the data table labeled correctly?
- Are the data reasonable?

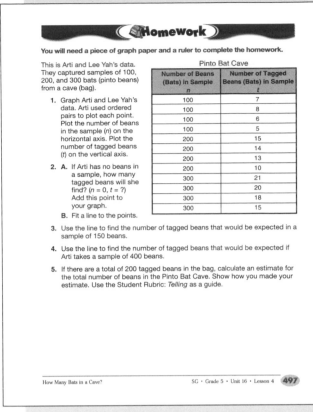

Student Guide - page 497 (Answers on p. 65)

Name _____ Date _____

PART 3 Making Brownies

Below is a list of ingredients Manny uses to make one batch of walnut crunch brownies.

Walnut Crunch Brownies
4 squares chocolate
$\frac{3}{4}$ cup butter
$1\frac{1}{2}$ cups sugar
4 eggs
1 teaspoon vanilla
$\frac{2}{3}$ cup flour
$\frac{1}{4}$ cup walnuts

1. Manny only has 2 eggs at home. He plans to make half a recipe. List how much of each ingredient he needs.

2. Manny shares his original recipe with Felicia. She plans to double the recipe. How much of each ingredient will she need?

PART 4 Geometry

1. The circumference of a circle is 32 cm. What is the diameter of the circle? Give your answer to the nearest tenth of a centimeter. (Use the π key on your calculator or use 3.14 for π.)

2. The radius of a circle is 4 cm. What is the circumference of the circle? Give your answer to the nearest tenth of a centimeter. (Use the π key on your calculator or use 3.14 for π.)

3. The length of a rectangle is 6 cm. Its area is 54 sq cm. What is its perimeter?

4. The perimeter of a square is 24 cm. What is the area of the square?

232 DAB · Grade 5 · Unit 16   BRINGING IT ALL TOGETHER: AN ASSESSMENT UNIT

Discovery Assignment Book - page 232 (Answers on p. 66)

Graphing the Data

- Does the graph have an appropriate title?
- Is the horizontal axis labeled correctly?
  (n–Total number of bats (beans) in a sample)
- Is the vertical axis labeled correctly?
  (t–Number of tagged bats (beans) in a sample)
- Are the axes scaled correctly?
- Are the points plotted correctly? Is the point (0, 0) included?
- Is the best-fit line drawn appropriately?
- Did students show on the graph how they used the best-fit line to write ratios?

Solving the Problems

- Are students' answers correct based on the data?
- Did students clearly show how they solved the problems?
- Did students solve the problems in more than one way?

Score **Question 11** using the Telling dimension of the *TIMS Multidimensional Rubric.* Encourage students to use the Student Rubric: *Telling* as a guide as they explain their solutions.

For more information on evaluating labs and scoring student work, see the Assessment section of the *Teacher Implementation Guide.*

Extension

- Students can check their estimates for the total population of beans in their bags using several methods. For example, they can measure the volume or capacity of all the beans in the bag. If one pound of beans is about 10 of the medium-size scoops used to collect the sample data, they can count the number of beans in one scoop and multiply this number by 10 to estimate the total number of beans in the whole bag.
- You can vary the size of the bat caves by giving some groups 2 pounds of beans in their bags. These groups should follow the same procedure. During class discussion, you can compare the two experiments by comparing the graphs, the ratios, and the estimates for the total number of beans in the bags.

Literature Connection

Stellaluna is an illustrated fictional story of a young bat that incorporates many facts about bats into the narrative.

At a Glance

Math Facts and Daily Practice and Problems

Assign DPP items I–N. Item I reviews the division facts. Items J and M involve computation. Item K practices finding the area of triangles. Task L and Challenge N involve problem solving.

Before the Lab

1. Students read and discuss the Adventure Book *Bats!*
2. Prepare a "bat cave" for each group of four students by placing 1 pound of baby lima beans in a self-closing bag.

Part 1. Preparing for the Lab, Tagging the Bats, and Sampling the Bat Population

1. Students read the Preparing for the Lab section in the *How Many Bats in a Cave?* Lab Pages in the *Student Guide*.
2. Students tag 250 beans from their bags and mix the tagged beans with the untagged beans.

Part 2. Drawing the Picture

1. Students draw a labeled picture of the lab. *(Question 1)*
2. Students answer *Questions 2–4.*

Part 3. Collecting the Data

Students pull four samples for each of three sizes of a scoop. For each of the 12 samples, they count the total number of beans and the number of tagged beans, recording the data in a table. *(Questions 5–6)*

Part 4. Graphing the Data

Students plot the data and draw a best-fit line. *(Question 7)*

Part 5. Exploring the Data

1. Students use the line to find and write ratios $(\frac{t}{n})$ for the number of tagged beans in a sample to the total number of beans in the sample. They examine the ratios to see if they are equal. *(Questions 8–10)*
2. Students use equal ratios to estimate the total number of beans in their bag. *(Question 11)*
3. Students check their estimates by using another method of estimation. (optional)

At a Glance

Homework

1. Assign the homework in the *Student Guide.* Students will need a piece of *Centimeter Graph Paper.*
2. Assign Parts 3 and 4 of the Home Practice.

Assessment

Choose one or more sections of the lab to use as an assessment.

Extension

1. Have students check their estimates for the total population in their bags by measuring the volume or capacity of the beans.
2. Vary the size of the bat caves by giving some groups 2 pounds of beans in their bags. Then compare the two experiments.

Connection

Read and discuss *Stellaluna* by Janell Cannon.

Answer Key is on pages 64–66.

Notes:

Name _____ Date _____

_____

Three-column Data Table, Blackline Master

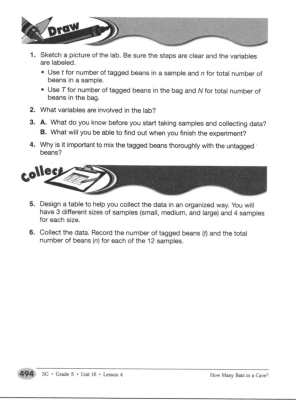

Student Guide - page 494

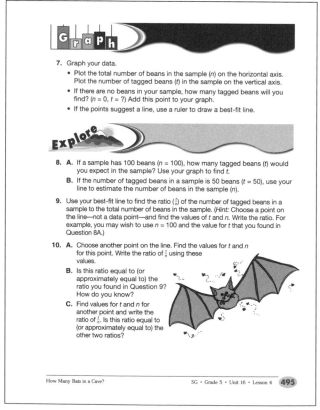

Student Guide - page 495

Student Guide (p. 494)

1. See Figure 3 in Lesson Guide 4 for a sample picture.*

2. The number of tagged beans in a sample *(t)*, total number of beans in the sample *(n)*, number of tagged beans in the bag *(T)*, and the total number of beans in the bag *(N)*.

3.* **A.** We know that the number of tagged beans in the bag *(T)* is 250.

   B. The total number of beans in the bag.

4. So the tagged beans will spread evenly and thus the same size samples will have approximately the same number of tagged beans.*

5.–6.* See Figure 4 in Lesson Guide 4 for a sample table.

Student Guide (p. 495)

7. See Figure 5 in the Lesson Guide for a sample graph.*

8.* **A.** Based on the sample graph given, $t = 20$ tagged beans

   B. Based on the sample graph given, $n = 245$ beans

9. $\frac{t}{n} = \frac{20 \text{ tagged beans}}{100 \text{ beans}} = \frac{1 \text{ tagged bean}}{5 \text{ beans}} = 0.20$*

10.* **A.** Points will vary. One possible ratio would be $\frac{t}{n} = \frac{33}{160}$

   B. Yes; $\frac{33 \text{ tagged beans}}{160 \text{ beans}} \approx 0.21$

   C. $\frac{t}{n} = \frac{42 \text{ tagged beans}}{200 \text{ beans}} \approx 0.21$

*Answers and/or discussion are included in the Lesson Guide.

Student Guide (p. 496)

11.* A. One possible strategy: $\dfrac{1 \text{ tagged bean}}{5 \text{ beans}} = \dfrac{250 \text{ tagged beans}}{N}$

    B. See Lesson Guide 4 for possible solution paths.

12. A. No. Taking more than one sample reduces the chances of error.

    B. Answers will vary.

---

11. **A.** Use a ratio from the line. Calculate an estimate for the total number of beans in your bag. That is, use equal ratios to find N.

$$\frac{\text{number of tagged beans in a sample } (t)}{\text{total number of beans in a sample } (n)} = \frac{\text{number of tagged beans in the bag } (T)}{\text{total number of beans in the bag } (N)}$$

$$\frac{t}{n} = \frac{250}{N}$$

    B. Explain how you made your estimate. Use the Student Rubric: *Telling* as a guide.

12. Look at the data in your table.

    A. If you had only taken one sample, would the data give you a good estimate for the total number of beans in your bag? Why or why not?

    B. You took four samples for each sample size. Do you recommend the same, more, or fewer samples? Why?

> **Bat Trivia**
>
> 🦇 The world's smallest mammal is the bumblebee bat of Thailand, weighing less than a penny.
>
> 🦇 Giant flying foxes that live in Indonesia have wingspans of nearly 6 feet.
>
> *Facts provided by Bat Conservation International*

496 SG • Grade 5 • Unit 16 • Lesson 4   How Many Bats in a Cave?

Student Guide - page 496

Student Guide (p. 497)

Homework

Solutions will vary slightly.

1.

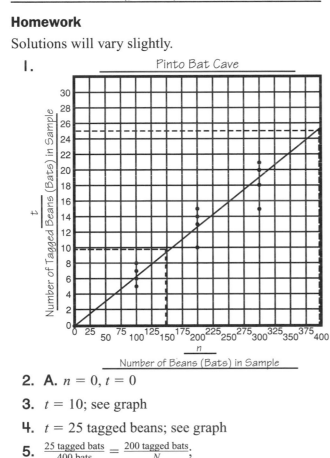

2. A. $n = 0$, $t = 0$

3. $t = 10$; see graph

4. $t = 25$ tagged beans; see graph

5. $\dfrac{25 \text{ tagged bats}}{400 \text{ bats}} = \dfrac{200 \text{ tagged bats}}{N}$,
    $N \approx 3200$

Homework

You will need a piece of graph paper and a ruler to complete the homework.

This is Arti and Lee Yah's data. They captured samples of 100, 200, and 300 bats (pinto beans) from a cave (bag).

Pinto Bat Cave

Number of Beans (Bats) in Sample n	Number of Tagged Beans (Bats) in Sample t
100	7
100	8
100	6
100	5
200	15
200	14
200	13
200	10
300	21
300	20
300	18
300	15

1. Graph Arti and Lee Yah's data. Arti used ordered pairs to plot each point. Plot the number of beans in the sample (n) on the horizontal axis. Plot the number of tagged beans (t) on the vertical axis.

2. **A.** If Arti has no beans in a sample, how many tagged beans will she find? ($n = 0$, $t = ?$) Add this point to your graph.

    B. Fit a line to the points.

3. Use the line to find the number of tagged beans that would be expected in a sample of 150 beans.

4. Use the line to find the number of tagged beans that would be expected if Arti takes a sample of 400 beans.

5. If there are a total of 200 tagged beans in the bag, calculate an estimate for the total number of beans in the Pinto Bat Cave. Show how you made your estimate. Use the Student Rubric: *Telling* as a guide.

How Many Bats in a Cave?   SG • Grade 5 • Unit 16 • Lesson 4 497

Student Guide - page 497

*Answers and/or discussion are included in the Lesson Guide.

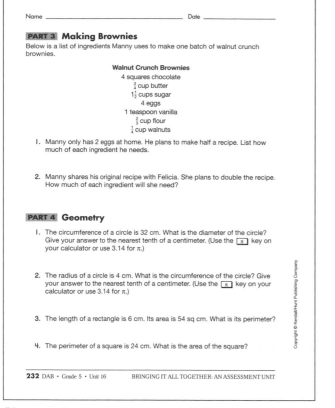

Discovery Assignment Book - page 232

Discovery Assignment Book (p. 232)

Home Practice*

Part 3. Making Brownies

1. 2 squares chocolate, $\frac{3}{8}$ cup butter, $\frac{3}{4}$ cup sugar, 2 eggs, $\frac{1}{2}$ teaspoon vanilla, $\frac{1}{3}$ cup flour, and $\frac{1}{8}$ cup walnuts.

2. 8 squares chocolate, $1\frac{1}{2}$ cups butter, 3 cups sugar, 8 eggs, 2 teaspoons vanilla, $1\frac{1}{3}$ cups flour, and $\frac{1}{2}$ cup walnuts.

Part 4. Geometry

1. $D = 10.2$ cm
2. $C = 25.1$ cm
3. Perimeter $= 30$ cm
4. Area $= 36$ sq cm

*Answers for all the Home Practice in the *Discovery Assignment Book* are at the end of the unit.

Lesson

5

Pattern Block Candy

Estimated Class Sessions **1-2**

Lesson Overview

In this assessment activity, students use pattern blocks to solve a problem involving numerical patterns. They write about their problem-solving strategies.

Key Content

- Identifying and describing number patterns.
- Using patterns to make predictions and solve problems.
- Solving open-response problems and communicating problem-solving strategies.
- Using the Student Rubric: *Solving* to self-assess problem-solving skills.

Math Facts

Complete DPP item O, which reviews the division facts.

Homework

Assign Part 5 of the Home Practice.

Assessment

Use the *TIMS Multidimensional Rubric* to score students' work. Encourage students to compare their work on this activity to similar activities in their portfolios.

Curriculum Sequence

Before This Unit

Students have solved open-response problems throughout the year. In particular, they collected data and used the patterns in the data to solve problems in Unit 2 Lesson 9 *Stack-Up.* They organized and displayed data in Unit 8 Lesson 4 *Florence Kelley's*

Report and used sampling techniques to make estimates in Unit 9 Lesson 6 *Grass Act.* More recently they described patterns in Unit 11 Lesson 3 *Patterns with Square Numbers* and Unit 11 Lesson 7 *A Further Look at Patterns and Primes.*

Materials List

Supplies and Copies

Student	Teacher
Supplies for Each Student	**Supplies**
• calculator • 1 set of pattern blocks (4 or 5 of each shape: red trapezoid, blue rhombus, green triangle, brown trapezoid, purple triangle)	
Copies	**Copies/Transparencies**
• 1 copy of *Pattern Block Candy* per student (*Unit Resource Guide* Pages 76–77)	• 1 transparency or poster of Student Rubric: *Solving*, optional (*Teacher Implementation Guide*, Assessment section) • 1 copy of *TIMS Multidimensional Rubric*, optional (*Teacher Implementation Guide*, Assessment section)

All blackline masters including assessment, transparency, and DPP masters are also on the Teacher Resource CD.

Student Books

Student Rubric: *Solving* (*Student Guide* Appendix B and Inside Back Cover)

Daily Practice and Problems and Home Practice

DPP items O–P (*Unit Resource Guide* Page 19)
Home Practice Part 5 (*Discovery Assignment Book* Page 233)

Note: Classrooms whose pacing differs significantly from the suggested pacing of the units should use the Math Facts Calendar in Section 4 of the *Facts Resource Guide* to ensure students receive the complete math facts program.

Assessment Tools

TIMS Multidimensional Rubric (*Teacher Implementation Guide,* Assessment section), optional

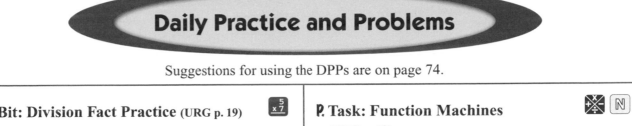

Daily Practice and Problems

Suggestions for using the DPPs are on page 74.

0. Bit: Division Fact Practice (URG p. 19) $\boxed{\times \frac{5}{7}}$

A. $6 \div 3 = n$ B. $25 \div 5 = n$

C. $n \div 3 = 9$ D. $20 \div n = 10$

E. $24 \div n = 4$ F. $n \div 8 = 8$

G. $54 \div 9 = n$ H. $15 \div 5 = n$

I. $n \div 4 = 8$ J. $n \div 10 = 7$

K. $14 \div n = 2$ L. $35 \div n = 7$

P. Task: Function Machines
(URG p. 19)

Complete the tables.

$q = (p - 2) \div 9$		$s = (r - 10) \div 7$		$u = (t + 1) \div 4$	
p	**q**	**r**	**s**	**t**	**u**
92			9	31	
83		59		27	
	7	52			5
47		38		15	
	3	24			3
	1	17		7	

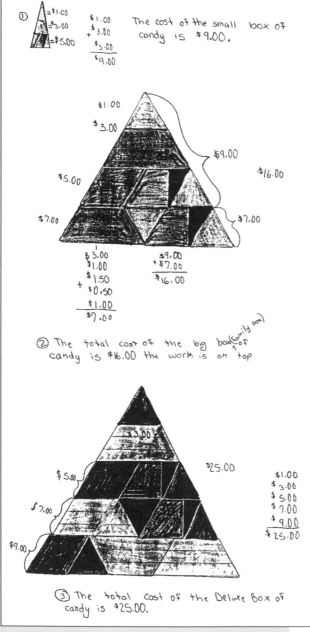

Figure 6: *Sample student work for Questions 1–3*

Before the Assessment

There are several ways to administer this assessment. Students can work in groups or individually for the whole assessment, or they can begin in groups to discuss strategies and then finish the assessment individually. For example, students can complete *Questions 1–3* with their groups and then complete *Questions 4–5* independently. You can then use the Solving dimension (or other dimensions) of the *TIMS Multidimensional Rubric* to score the work that is completed independently.

Teaching the Assessment

Note: This activity is an adaption from *Activity 5: There Are Pattern Blocks in My Cake!* in the NCTM Grades 5–8 Addenda Series. Reprinted with permission from *Understanding Rational Numbers and Proportions,* copyright 1994 by the National Council of Teachers of Mathematics.

Begin this activity by reading the *Pattern Block Candy* Assessment Pages from the *Unit Resource Guide* to ensure that each group understands the context of the problem. To help students more clearly understand the expectations of the problem, review the student version of the rubrics that you will use to score their work.

When students begin their group discussions, they should work without consulting you and instead rely on group members to help them with their questions. If a group needs additional guidance from you to get started, note this so you can include this information in your evaluation of their abilities to solve problems.

Once each group completes the questions they are to do together, students complete the remaining questions independently. Before scoring their work, give them an opportunity to revise it based on your input. Refer to the student rubrics as you make comments. For example, you may ask a student to explain a strategy more clearly, organize his or her work in a table, or look back at a solution to see if it makes sense.

Sample student work for *Questions 1–3* is shown in Figure 6. Note that this student (whom we call Student A) organized the cost of each flavor of candy in a data table. She also clearly showed how she found the cost of each box of candy.

To assist you in scoring student work, specific questions are listed below for the Solving dimension of the rubric:

Solving

- Did students clearly understand the relationship between the elements of the problem? For example, did they understand and use the relationship between the size of the pattern blocks and their cost? Did they understand the relationship between the number of rows of candy in a box and the total cost of the box?

- Did students use efficient problem-solving strategies? For example, did they find a more efficient strategy than drawing a box with 8 rows and finding the cost of each row to answer **Question 4?**

- Did students organize their data? For example, did they use a chart to show the cost of each type of candy? Did they use pictures and data tables?

- Did students connect the patterns in this problem to patterns from previous problems? For example, the patterns in this problem are similar to the patterns in Unit 11 Lesson 3 *Patterns with Square Numbers.*

- Did students continue to work on the problem until they arrived at a solution?

- Did students look back and make sure their solutions were reasonable based on the data they gathered?

Three student responses to **Questions 4–5** follow. Their work has been scored using the Solving dimension of the *TIMS Multidimensional Rubric*. Student A's work is a continuation of the work in Figure 6.

Student A's work

Student A's work scored on the Solving dimension

Solving	Level 4	Level 3	Level 2	Level 1
Identifies the elements of the problem and their relationships to one another	All major elements identified ✗	Most elements identified	Some, but shows little understanding of relationships	Few or none
Uses problem-solving strategies which are…	Systematic, complete, efficient, and possibly elegant ✗	Systematic and nearly complete, but not efficient	Incomplete or unsystematic	Not evident or inappropriate
Organizes relevant information…	Systematically and efficiently ✗	Systematically, with minor errors	Unsystematically	Not at all
Relates the problem and solution to previously encountered mathematics and makes connections that are…	At length, elegant, and meaningful	Evident ✗	Brief or logically unsound	Not evident
Persists in the problem-solving process…	At length	Until a solution is reached ✗	Briefly	Not at all
Looks back to examine the reasonableness of the solution and draws conclusions that are…	Insightful and comprehensive	Correct ✗	Incorrect or logically unsound	Not present

Figure 7: *Student A's work and score*

Student A scored a 3 on the Solving dimension. She showed that she understood the elements of the problem by setting up a table and identifying patterns that helped her solve the problems efficiently. Information is organized systematically in a table, and she also clearly shows the calculator keystrokes she used to compute. She persisted in the problem-solving process until she found a solution, but she did not earn a 4 because she did not look for an alternative solution that would examine the reasonableness of her solution.

Student B scored a 2 on the Solving dimension. He understood enough of the problem to be able to draw candy boxes and correctly compute the cost of the boxes. However, he did not demonstrate that he was able to find the patterns that could help him solve *Questions 4–5* efficiently. To solve *Question 4,* he simply drew a box with 8 rows and calculated the total cost. He was not able to apply any patterns to develop a more efficient strategy. The information in the table, while correct, is not well organized. He gave us no information on how he found the patterns he used in *Question 5.* He persisted in the problem-solving process until he found one solution to each problem, but he showed no evidence that he looked back at his solutions to see if they were reasonable or to devise a second strategy to check his first solution.

Student B's work

4. The box of eight rows cost $64.00.

First I drew a picture of eight rows of a box then I found how much each rows cost then I did a table then I add the first row and it gave me $15.00 then I added $49.00 to give me $64.00

shapes	
Green triangle	$3000
blue Rhombus	$6.00
Red trapezord	$6.00
	15.00
	13.00
	11.00
	9.00
	7.00
	5.00
	3.00
	1.00
	64.00

5. First I did a eenation and the eenation is this: $50^2 = 2,500$ that's how much the box of 50 rows is going to cost. I discoveries because each of the row is adding 2 that's the pattern we discovered.

Student B's work scored on the Solving dimension

Solving	Level 4	Level 3	Level 2	Level 1
Identifies the elements of the problem and their relationships to one another	All major elements identified	Most elements identified	Some, but shows little understand-ing of relationships	Few or none
Uses problem-solving strategies which are…	Systematic, com-plete, efficient, and possibly elegant	Systematic and nearly complete, but not efficient	Incomplete or unsystematic	Not evident or inappropriate
Organizes relevant information…	Systematically and efficiently	Systematically, with minor errors	Unsystematically	Not at all
Relates the problem and solution to previously encountered mathematics and makes connections that are…	At length, elegant, and meaningful	Evident	Brief or logically unsound	Not evident
Persists in the problem-solving process…	At length	Until a solution is reached	Briefly	Not at all
Looks back to examine the reasonableness of the solution and draws conclusions that are…	Insightful and comprehensive	Correct	Incorrect or logically unsound	Not present

Figure 8: *Student B's work and score*

Student C's work

1	$1.00
2	$3.00
3	$5.00 ↑
4	$7.00
5	$9.00 } add up
6	$11.00
7	$13.00
8	$15.00
9	$17.00
10	$19.00

4) $\overset{3}{1}5.00$ = 8 row   The extra large box
13.00 = 7 row   cost $64.00.
11.00 = 6 row
9.00 = 5 row   I Know this because
7.00 = 4 row   I organized my data
5.00 = 3 row   in a data table.
* 3.00 = 2 row
  1.00 = 1 row
$64.00

5) Rule.
50 x 2 - 1 = 99

The special box cost $2500.

I Know this because in
the cost side I add 2 but
instead of adding 2 I subtract
2 from $99 to get the cost of
the hole extra Deluxe box.

work. [symbol] key strokes.

Not all of Student C's work is included here. On his paper he showed over 200 calculator keystrokes that he used to compute the cost of the Valentine's Day box. He began with 99 (the cost in dollars of the fiftieth row). Then, he subtracted 2 from the cost of this row to find the cost of the next smallest row. He added the cost of both rows together and began a running total in the calculator's memory of the total cost of the rows. By subtracting 2 from the cost of each smaller row and adding the new cost to the running total, he was able to find the cost of a box with 50 rows.

However, this is too much work and if you use My rule all you have to do is this. Look at a box of two rows. the cost is 3.00 + 1.00 = 4.00. If you square the row Number, $2^2 = 4.00$ the cost of the box. Try it for a box of 5 rows and see if the Patterns works. Row 5+4+3+2+1=$25.00. Square row 5 ($5^2 = 25$) you got the same Result. Try it For all the other rows and it will work.

Finally a box of 50 rows will cost [50 x 5 2,500]. ///.

Student C's work scored on the Solving dimension

Solving	Level 4	Level 3	Level 2	Level 1
Identifies the elements of the problem and their relationships to one another	All major elements identified ╳	Most elements identified	Some, but shows little understanding of relationships	Few or none
Uses problem-solving strategies which are…	Systematic, complete, efficient, and possibly elegant ╳	Systematic and nearly complete, but not efficient	Incomplete or unsystematic	Not evident or inappropriate
Organizes relevant information…	Systematically and efficiently	╳(Systematically, with minor errors)	Unsystematically	Not at all
Relates the problem and solution to previously encountered mathematics and makes connections that are…	At length, elegant, and meaningful	Evident ╳	Brief or logically unsound	Not evident
Persists in the problem-solving process…	At length ╳	Until a solution is reached	Briefly	Not at all
Looks back to examine the reasonableness of the solution and draws conclusions that are…	Insightful and comprehensive ╳	Correct	Incorrect or logically unsound	Not present

Figure 9: *Student C's work and score*

Student C scored a 4. He showed that he understood the elements of the problem by using patterns to solve the problem systematically and completely. However, he does not give us all the information we need to show how he found the pattern he used to make his calculations. He persisted in the problem-solving process until he found two solutions to the problem and compared the results.

Journal Prompt

Explain how your group worked together to solve this problem. What role did each group member take? How did you work together to answer the questions?

Math Facts

DPP item O reviews the division facts using variables.

Homework and Practice

- Assign DPP item P, which involves completing function machine tables.
- Assign Part 5 of the Home Practice, which practices computation with whole numbers and fractions.

Answers for Part 5 of the Home Practice are in the Answer Key at the end of this lesson and at the end of this unit.

Assessment

Once you score and return students' work, ask them to review all the open-response assessment problems in their portfolios that they completed this year. Encourage students to compare work from the beginning of the year to their work on this problem and write about their growth. They can use the rubrics that were used to score each problem to help them talk about the growth. For example, a student may write that he or she uses tables to organize data more often now than at the start of the year.

Resource

This problem was adapted from Activity 5 on Page 19 of *Understanding Rational Numbers and Proportions,* copyright 1994 by the National Council of Teachers of Mathematics. All rights reserved.

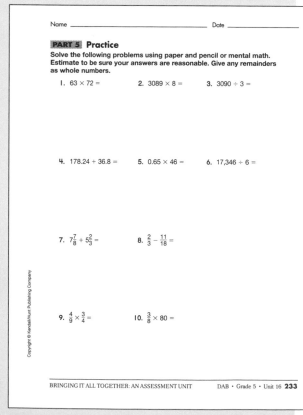

Name _____ Date _____

PART 5 **Practice**

Solve the following problems using paper and pencil or mental math. Estimate to be sure your answers are reasonable. Give any remainders as whole numbers.

1. $63 \times 72 =$　　2. $3089 \times 8 =$　　3. $3090 \div 3 =$

4. $178.24 + 36.8 =$　　5. $0.65 \times 46 =$　　6. $17,346 \div 6 =$

7. $7\frac{7}{8} + 5\frac{2}{3} =$　　8. $\frac{2}{3} - \frac{11}{18} =$

9. $\frac{4}{9} \times \frac{3}{4} =$　　10. $\frac{3}{8} \times 80 =$

BRINGING IT ALL TOGETHER: AN ASSESSMENT UNIT　　　DAB • Grade 5 • Unit 16 **233**

Discovery Assignment Book - page 233 (Answers on p. 78)

At a Glance

Math Facts and Daily Practice and Problems

Complete DPP items O–P. Item O reviews the division facts. Item P reviews functions.

Teaching the Assessment

1. Distribute pattern blocks. Calculators should be available.
2. Read the opening paragraph on the *Pattern Block Candy* Assessment Pages in the *Unit Resource Guide*.
3. Review the student rubrics you will use to score student work.
4. Students complete *Questions 1–3* with their groups.
5. Students complete *Questions 4–5* independently and write about their strategies.
6. Provide feedback on student work.
7. Students revise their work based on your input.
8. Students score their work using the *TIMS Multidimensional Rubric* and compare it to other problems completed earlier in the year.

Homework

Assign Part 5 of the Home Practice.

Assessment

Use the *TIMS Multidimensional Rubric* to score students' work. Encourage students to compare their work on this activity to similar activities in their portfolios.

Answer Key is on page 78.

Notes:

Pattern Block Candy

The TIMS Candy Company is selling boxes of candy. The candy is boxed in triangular-shaped boxes. Each flavor of candy is a different shape. The shapes and sizes of the candy are the same shapes and sizes as pattern blocks. For example, 2 green triangles (chocolate mint) equal 1 blue rhombus (blueberry creme).

Chocolate Mint   Blueberry Creme

Pattern Block Candy

Candy Flavor	Shapes
Mint Chocolate	Green Triangle
Raspberry Creme	Purple Triangle
Nut Clusters	Brown Trapezoid
Cherry Creme	Red Trapezoid
Blueberry Creme	Blue Rhombus

Mr. Haddad, the owner of the TIMS Candy Company, needs to set prices. The cost of each type of candy is based on its size. Each Mint Chocolate (green triangle) costs $1.00, so each Blueberry Creme (blue rhombus) costs $2.00, each Raspberry Creme (purple triangle) costs $.50.

Solve the following problems. Use pattern blocks to help you. Record your work on a separate sheet of paper.

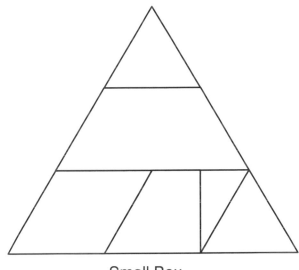

Small Box

1. The cost of a box of candy is based on its size. The total cost of the box is the total cost of the pieces of candy in the box. The Small Box shown here has three rows of candy. Find the cost of the Small Box.

2. Mr. Haddad sells different-sized boxes. A Family Box has 4 rows of candy in a triangular-shaped box.

   A. Use pattern blocks to build a Family Box of candy. (*Hint:* You can add to the Small Box. There are many different possible ways to build a Family Box.) Make a drawing of your Family Box.

   B. Find the cost of each row in your Family Box. Show all your work.

   C. Find the total cost of the box.

3. The Deluxe Box has 5 rows.

   A. Use pattern blocks to build a Deluxe Box of candy. Make a drawing of your Deluxe Box. (*Hint:* You can add to your Family Box.)

   B. Find the cost of each row of your Deluxe Box. Show all your work.

   C. Find the total cost of your Deluxe Box.

To solve Questions 4–5, choose from the tools and strategies you have used in math class. Tools you may find helpful are pattern blocks and calculators. Strategies you may find helpful include drawing pictures, making data tables, and looking for patterns. Use the Student Rubric: *Solving* to guide your work.

4. Mr. Haddad plans to sell an Extra Large Box with 8 rows of candy. Find the total cost of an Extra Large Box. Explain your solution strategies.

5. On Valentine's Day the TIMS Candy Company sells a special box with 50 rows of candy. Find the total cost of this special box. Explain your solution strategies.

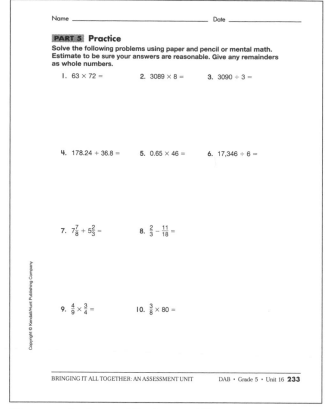

Discovery Assignment Book - page 233

Discovery Assignment Book (p. 233)

Home Practice*

Part 5. Practice

1. 4536
2. 24,712
3. 1030
4. 215.04
5. 29.9
6. 2891
7. $13\frac{13}{24}$
8. $\frac{1}{18}$
9. $\frac{1}{3}$
10. 30

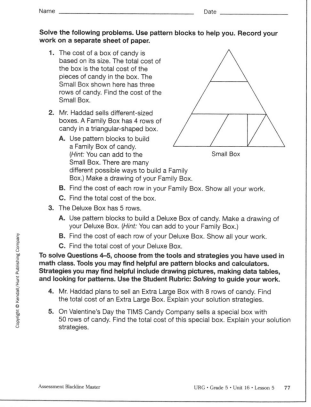

Unit Resource Guide - page 77

Unit Resource Guide (p. 77)

1. $9†
2. **A.** Answers will vary.†
   B. $1, $3, $5, $7
   C. $16
3. **A.** Answers will vary.†
   B. $1, $3, $5, $7, $9
   C. $25
4. $64. See student work in Lesson Guide 5 for strategies.†
5. $50^2 = $2500. See student work in Lesson Guide 5 for strategies.†

*Answers for all the Home Practice in the *Discovery Assignment Book* are at the end of the unit.
†Answers and/or discussion are included in the Lesson Guide.

Lesson 6

End-of-Year Test

Estimated Class Sessions

1-2

Lesson Overview

Students take a test consisting of short items that test skills and concepts learned in the last quarter of the year.

Key Content

• Assessing skills and concepts from Units 13–16.

Assessment

1. Students solve the problems on the *End-of-Year Test* using tools available to them in the classroom.
2. Assign Part 6 of the Home Practice.

Materials List

Supplies and Copies

Student	Teacher
Supplies for Each Student • ruler • protractor • compass • calculator	**Supplies**

Copies
 	
• 1 copy of *End-of-Year Test* per student
  (*Unit Resource Guide* Pages 83–87)
• 1 copy of *Centimeter Dot Paper* per student
  (*Unit Resource Guide* Page 88)
	Copies/Transparencies

All blackline masters including assessment, transparency, and DPP masters are also on the Teacher Resource CD.

Daily Practice and Problems and Home Practice

DPP items Q–R (*Unit Resource Guide* Pages 19–20)
Home Practice Part 6 (*Discovery Assignment Book* Page 234)

Note: Classrooms whose pacing differs significantly from the suggested pacing of the units should use the Math Facts Calendar in Section 4 of the *Facts Resource Guide* to ensure students receive the complete math facts program.

Daily Practice and Problems

Suggestions for using the DPPs are on page 81.

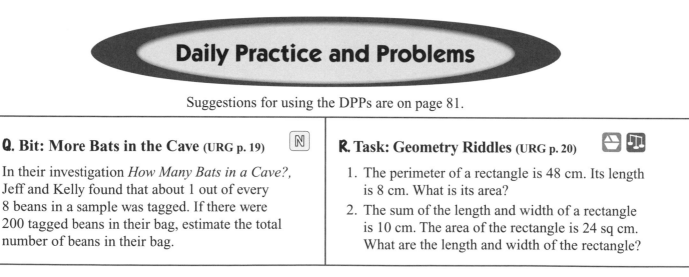

Q. Bit: More Bats in the Cave (URG p. 19)

In their investigation *How Many Bats in a Cave?*, Jeff and Kelly found that about 1 out of every 8 beans in a sample was tagged. If there were 200 tagged beans in their bag, estimate the total number of beans in their bag.

R. Task: Geometry Riddles (URG p. 20)

1. The perimeter of a rectangle is 48 cm. Its length is 8 cm. What is its area?
2. The sum of the length and width of a rectangle is 10 cm. The area of the rectangle is 24 sq cm. What are the length and width of the rectangle?

Teaching the Activity

A set of short items from Units 13, 14, 15, and 16 are provided for you to build a test appropriate for your class. Choose items from the units you covered in class. Students take this test independently. It is designed to take one class period; however, you may wish to allow more time if needed. Students should complete Part 1 of the test without a calculator. They should use the tools available to them in the classroom to complete Part 2, including protractors, rulers, compasses, and calculators. Students will need *Centimeter Dot Paper* to complete **Question 10.**

Students should follow the directions for each item. Remind them to be clear and concise when describing their problem-solving strategies.

Homework and Practice

Assign DPP items Q and R. Bit Q reviews proportions and Task R explores perimeter and area of rectangles.

Assessment

- Assign the *End-of-Year Test.*
- Use the problems in Part 6 of the Home Practice to assess students' problem-solving abilities.

Answers for Part 6 of the Home Practice are in the Answer Key at the end of this lesson and at the end of this unit.

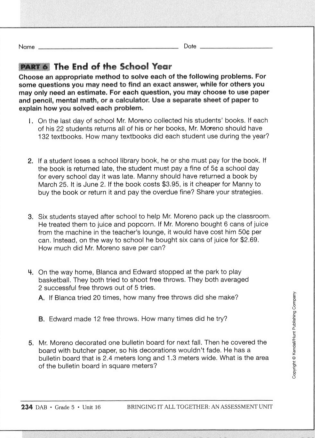

Name _____ Date _____

PART 6 **The End of the School Year**

Choose an appropriate method to solve each of the following problems. For some questions you may need to find an exact answer, while for others you may only need an estimate. For each question, you may choose to use paper and pencil, mental math, or a calculator. Use a separate sheet of paper to explain how you solved each problem.

1. On the last day of school Mr. Moreno collected his students' books. If each of his 22 students returns all of his or her books, Mr. Moreno should have 132 textbooks. How many textbooks did each student use during the year?

2. If a student loses a school library book, he or she must pay for the book. If the book is returned late, the student must pay a fine of 5¢ a school day for every school day it was late. Manny should have returned a book by March 25. It is June 2. If the book costs $3.95, is it cheaper for Manny to buy the book or return it and pay the overdue fine? Share your strategies.

3. Six students stayed after school to help Mr. Moreno pack up the classroom. He treated them to juice and popcorn. If Mr. Moreno bought 6 cans of juice from the machine in the teacher's lounge, it would have cost him 50¢ per can. Instead, on the way to school he bought six cans of juice for $2.69. How much did Mr. Moreno save per can?

4. On the way home, Blanca and Edward stopped at the park to play basketball. They both tried to shoot free throws. They both averaged 2 successful free throws out of 5 tries.
   A. If Blanca tried 20 times, how many free throws did she make?

   B. Edward made 12 free throws. How many times did he try?

5. Mr. Moreno decorated one bulletin board for next fall. Then he covered the board with butcher paper, so his decorations wouldn't fade. He has a bulletin board that is 2.4 meters long and 1.3 meters wide. What is the area of the bulletin board in square meters?

234 DAB • Grade 5 • Unit 16   BRINGING IT ALL TOGETHER: AN ASSESSMENT UNIT

Discovery Assignment Book - page 234 (Answers on p. 89)

Math Facts and Daily Practice and Problems

Complete DPP items Q–R. Item Q reviews proportions in the context of populations and samples. Item R reviews area and perimeter.

Teaching the Assessment

1. Students solve the problems on the *End-of-Year Test* using tools available to them in the classroom.
2. Assign Part 6 of the Home Practice.

Answer Key is on pages 89–91.

Notes:

End-of-Year Test

Part 1

Solve the following problem without a calculator.

1. **A.** Find the area of a rectangle that is 19.5 cm by 7 cm.

   B. Find the perimeter.

Name _____ Date _____

Part 2

Complete each of the following questions. You will need a ruler, a compass, a protractor, a calculator, and one sheet of *Centimeter Dot Paper* to complete this part of the test.

2. A circle has a diameter of 126 feet. Find the circumference of this circle. Show your work. Round your answer to the nearest whole foot.

3. **A.** Construct a triangle with sides 5 centimeters, 8 centimeters, and 10 centimeters in length.

   B. Find the measures of the angles._____ _____ _____

4. A circle has a circumference of 15 centimeters. Find the diameter of the circle. Show your work. Round your answer to the nearest tenth of a centimeter.

Assessment Blackline Master

5. An object has a mass of 56 grams and a volume of 8 cc. What is the volume of an object made of the same material whose mass is 28 grams?

6. An object has a mass of 50 grams and a volume of 88 cc. Will it sink or float in water? Why? (*Hint:* The density of water is $\frac{1g}{1cc}$.)

7. At the dog show, 3 of the winning dogs were small dogs and 5 were large dogs. There were 8 winning dogs in all.

   A. Write a ratio comparing the number of small dogs to the number of large dogs. Be sure to label your ratio.

   B. Write a ratio comparing the number of large dogs to the total number of winners. Be sure to label your ratio.

8. On the map of Ourtown, the scale shows that 2 cm represents 3 miles. On the map, the distance from the zoo to the beach is 8 cm. Write a proportion and solve it to find the actual distance from the zoo to the beach in miles.

9. A. Mr. Goodhammer is building a rectangular platform for a school play. He must build a platform with an area of 72 sq ft. The lengths of each side are whole numbers of feet. What are the lengths of the sides of all the possible platforms Mr. Goodhammer can make?

B. Can this platform be a square? Explain your thinking.

Record your answers for Question 10 on dot paper.

10. Make two triangles that are not congruent. Draw both triangles so that they have a base of 8 units and a height of 5 units. Find the area of each triangle.

Use the following circle graph to answer Questions 11–13. The graph shows the percentages of $1 bills, $2 bills, $5 bills, etc., in use in the United States in 1994.

Bills in Use, 1994

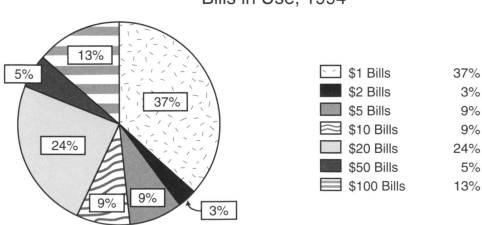

$1 Bills	37%
$2 Bills	3%
$5 Bills	9%
$10 Bills	9%
$20 Bills	24%
$50 Bills	5%
$100 Bills	13%

Copyright © Kendall/Hunt Publishing Company

11. Which 2 types of bills made up about 50% of the bills in use in 1994?

12. Which type of bill had the smallest percentage of the bills in use in 1994?

13. Which type of bill made up about $\frac{1}{4}$ of the total bills in use in 1994?

14. Shannon made the circle graph below. However, she forgot to label each part of the graph, and her data table is not complete. Complete her data table and then label each part of her circle graph.

What's in Our Landfills

Type of Trash	Fraction	Decimal	Percent
Metal	$\frac{3}{50}$		
Food/Yard		0.13	
Plastic	$\frac{1}{10}$		
Paper	$\frac{1}{2}$		
Other Trash			21%

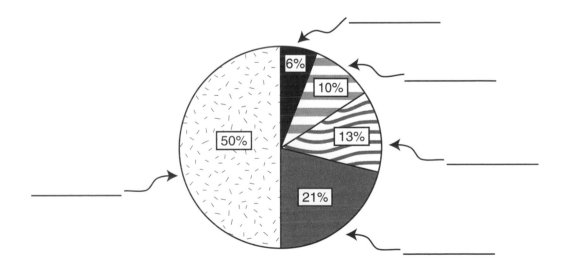

Centimeter Dot Paper

Blackline Master

Discovery Assignment Book (p. 234)

Home Practice*

Part 6. The End of the School Year

1. 6 textbooks

2. Pay the overdue fines. Strategies will vary.

3. About a nickel per can

4. **A.** 8

   B. 30

5. 3.12 sq m

Name _____ Date _____

PART 6 The End of the School Year

Choose an appropriate method to solve each of the following problems. For some questions you may need to find an exact answer, while for others you may only need an estimate. For each question, you may choose to use paper and pencil, mental math, or a calculator. Use a separate sheet of paper to explain how you solved each problem.

1. On the last day of school Mr. Moreno collected his students' books. If each of his 22 students returns all of his or her books, Mr. Moreno should have 132 textbooks. How many textbooks did each student use during the year?

2. If a student loses a school library book, he or she must pay for the book. If the book is returned late, the student must pay a fine of 5¢ a school day for every school day it was late. Manny should have returned a book by March 25. It is June 2. If the book costs $3.95, is it cheaper for Manny to buy the book or return it and pay the overdue fine? Share your strategies.

3. Six students stayed after school to help Mr. Moreno pack up the classroom. He treated them to juice and popcorn. If Mr. Moreno bought 6 cans of juice from the machine in the teacher's lounge, it would have cost him 50¢ per can. Instead, on the way to school he bought six cans of juice for $2.69. How much did Mr. Moreno save per can?

4. On the way home, Blanca and Edward stopped at the park to play basketball. They both tried to shoot free throws. They both averaged 2 successful free throws out of 5 tries.

   A. If Blanca tried 20 times, how many free throws did she make?

   B. Edward made 12 free throws. How many times did he try?

5. Mr. Moreno decorated one bulletin board for next fall. Then he covered the board with butcher paper, so his decorations wouldn't fade. He has a bulletin board that is 2.4 meters long and 1.3 meters wide. What is the area of the bulletin board in square meters?

234 DAB · Grade 5 · Unit 16   BRINGING IT ALL TOGETHER: AN ASSESSMENT UNIT

Discovery Assignment Book - page 234

Unit Resource Guide (p. 83)

End-of-Year Test

1. **A.** 136.5 sq cm

   B. 53 cm

Name _____ Date _____

End-of-Year Test

Part 1

Solve the following problem without a calculator.

1. **A.** Find the area of a rectangle that is 19.5 cm by 7 cm.

   B. Find the perimeter.

Assessment Blackline Master   URG · Grade 5 · Unit 16 · Lesson 6   83

Unit Resource Guide - page 83

*Answers for all the Home Practice in the *Discovery Assignment Book* are at the end of the unit.

Name _____ Date _____

Part 2

Complete each of the following questions. You will need a ruler, a compass, a protractor, a calculator, and one sheet of *Centimeter Dot Paper* to complete this part of the test.

2. A circle has a diameter of 126 feet. Find the circumference of this circle. Show your work. Round your answer to the nearest whole foot.

3. **A.** Construct a triangle with sides 5 centimeters, 8 centimeters, and 10 centimeters in length.

    B. Find the measures of the angles. _____ _____ _____

4. A circle has a circumference of 15 centimeters. Find the diameter of the circle. Show your work. Round your answer to the nearest tenth of a centimeter.

Unit Resource Guide - page 84

Unit Resource Guide (p. 84)

2. $C = \pi \times D = \pi \times 126$ feet ≈ 396 feet

3. **A.**

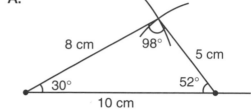

    B. $30°, 52°, 98°$

4. $D = C \div \pi = 15$ cm$/\pi = 4.8$ cm

Name _____ Date _____

5. An object has a mass of 56 grams and a volume of 8 cc. What is the volume of an object made of the same material whose mass is 28 grams?

6. An object has a mass of 50 grams and a volume of 88 cc. Will it sink or float in water? Why? (*Hint:* The density of water is $\frac{1g}{1cc}$.)

7. At the dog show, 3 of the winning dogs were small dogs and 5 were large dogs. There were 8 winning dogs in all.

    A. Write a ratio comparing the number of small dogs to the number of large dogs. Be sure to label your ratio.

    B. Write a ratio comparing the number of large dogs to the total number of winners. Be sure to label your ratio.

8. On the map of Ourtown, the scale shows that 2 cm represents 3 miles. On the map, the distance from the zoo to the beach is 8 cm. Write a proportion and solve it to find the actual distance from the zoo to the beach in miles.

Unit Resource Guide - page 85

Unit Resource Guide (p. 85)

5. $\frac{28 \text{ grams}}{V} = \frac{56 \text{ grams}}{8 \text{ cc}}$; $V = 4$ cc

6. Density of the object $= \frac{50 \text{ grams}}{88 \text{ cc}} = 0.57$ grams/cc. Since the density of the object is less than the density of water, the object will float in water.

7. **A.** $\frac{3 \text{ small dogs}}{5 \text{ large dogs}}$

    B. $\frac{5 \text{ large dogs}}{8 \text{ winning dogs}}$

8. $\frac{3 \text{ miles}}{2 \text{ cm}} = \frac{D}{8 \text{ cm}}$; $D = 12$ miles

---

Unit Resource Guide (p. 86)

9. **A.** 1 ft × 72 ft, 2 ft × 36 ft, 3 ft × 24 ft, 4 ft × 18 ft, 6 ft × 12 ft, and 8 ft × 9 ft

   B. No. Since 72 is not a square number, the stage cannot be a square.

10. Area of both triangles is $\frac{1}{2} \times 5 \times 8 = 20$ sq cm.

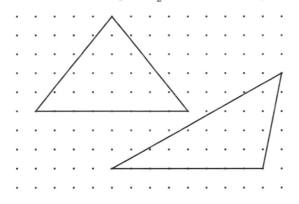

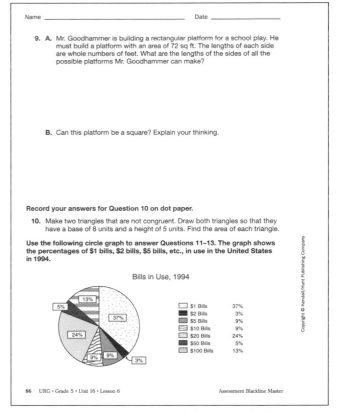

Unit Resource Guide - page 86

Unit Resource Guide (p. 87)

11. $1 and $100 bills

12. $2 bills

13. $20 bills

14.

Type of Trash	Fraction	Decimal	Percent
Metal	$\frac{3}{50}$	0.06	6%
Food/Yard	$\frac{13}{100}$	0.13	13%
Plastic	$\frac{1}{10}$	0.1	10%
Paper	$\frac{1}{2}$	0.5	50%
Other Trash	$\frac{21}{100}$	0.21	21%

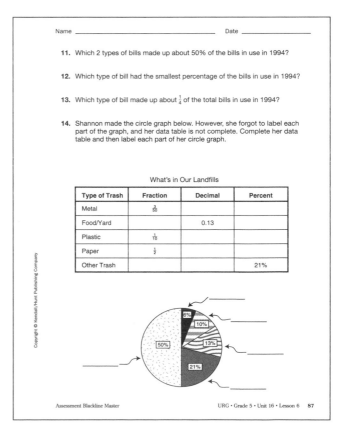

Unit Resource Guide - page 87

Lesson 7

Portfolio Review

Lesson Overview

Estimated Class Sessions

1

Students review the work they have collected and decide which pieces they will include in their portfolios. Students look for work that shows their growth over the school year.

Key Content

- Organizing work in a portfolio.
- Using portfolios to self-assess mathematical growth.

Math Facts

Complete DPP item S, which involves finding a pattern in a data table and continuing it.

Assessment

Transfer appropriate documentation from the Unit 16 *Observational Assessment Record* to students' *Individual Assessment Record Sheets*.

Materials List

Supplies and Copies

Student	Teacher
Supplies for Each Student • collection folder • portfolio folder	**Supplies**
Copies	**Copies/Transparencies**

All blackline masters including assessment, transparency, and DPP masters are also on the Teacher Resource CD.

Student Books

Portfolio Review (*Student Guide* Pages 498–499)

Daily Practice and Problems and Home Practice

DPP items S–T (*Unit Resource Guide* Pages 20–21)

Note: Classrooms whose pacing differs significantly from the suggested pacing of the units should use the Math Facts Calendar in Section 4 of the *Facts Resource Guide* to ensure students receive the complete math facts program.

Assessment Tools

Observational Assessment Record (*Unit Resource Guide* Pages 9–10)
Individual Assessment Record Sheet (*Teacher Implementation Guide*, Assessment section)

S. Bit: Mental Math (URG p. 20)

Use mental math and patterns to complete the following table. Tell the rule for the table.

Input	Output
0	1
1	6
2	11
	21
7	
11	
	26

T. Task: Peanut Butter Cookies
(URG p. 21)

Here are the ingredients for a peanut butter cookie recipe.

$\frac{3}{4}$ cup brown sugar $\frac{3}{4}$ cup white sugar

1 cup peanut butter $\frac{1}{3}$ cup shortening

$\frac{1}{3}$ cup butter $\frac{1}{2}$ tsp. baking powder

1 tsp. baking soda   2 eggs

$2\frac{1}{2}$ cups flour   1 tsp. vanilla

1. It's Arti's birthday. She wants to bring cookies to school. She needs to double the ingredients to make two batches of cookies. List each ingredient and how much Arti needs of each.

2. If the recipe is tripled, how much of each ingredient will Arti need?

Teaching the Activity

Read the first page of the *Portfolio Review* Activity Pages in the *Student Guide*. Review the purpose and the focus of the portfolios as established earlier in your classroom. Discuss the types of pieces and the number of pieces that students should include in their final portfolios.

Use **Question 1** in the Explore section of the *Student Guide* to help students choose appropriate items from their collection folders to add to their portfolios. **Questions 2–3** suggest that students place the *Experiment Review Chart* from Lesson 1 in their portfolios along with one or two other pieces of work from this unit. **Question 4** reminds students to update their table of contents at this time. **Question 5** asks students to write a paragraph comparing a piece of work they completed at the beginning of the year to one they completed recently. **Question 6** asks students to write about their favorite piece of work.

Give students an opportunity to celebrate the accomplishments that their portfolios represent. Since this is the last opportunity they will have to share their portfolios, you may want to make time for students to present their portfolios within the classroom. One way to do this is to have students work in pairs. Students can then present the pieces they selected for their portfolios, and explain why they made the choices they did. Students can also present the one piece they feel best represents their growth this year.

Homework and Practice

Assign DPP item S, which reviews patterns, and Task T, which reviews fractions in the context of a recipe.

Assessment

Transfer appropriate documentation from the Unit 16 *Observational Assessment Record* to students' *Individual Assessment Record Sheets*.

Student Guide - page 498

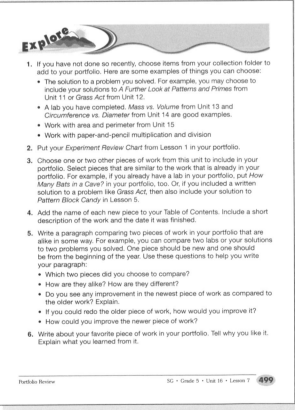

Student Guide - page 499

At a Glance

Math Facts and Daily Practice and Problems

Complete DPP items S–T. Item S involves finding a pattern in a data table and continuing it. Task T reviews fractions in a recipe.

Teaching the Activity

1. Read together the vignette on the *Portfolio Review* Activity Pages in the *Student Guide*.
2. Review the purpose and the focus of the portfolios that you established in your classroom.
3. Review the type and number of pieces to include.
4. Review the work in the collection folder for activities and labs to include in the portfolio.
5. Use *Questions 1–3* to help students choose appropriate items from their collection folders to add to their portfolios.
6. *Question 4* reminds students to update their Table of Contents.
7. Students write a paragraph comparing two pieces of work. *(Question 5)*
8. Students write about their favorite piece of work. *(Question 6)*
9. Students share their portfolios and present one piece they feel best represents their growth this year.

Assessment

Transfer appropriate documentation from the Unit 16 *Observational Assessment Record* to students' *Individual Assessment Record Sheets*.

Notes:

Discovery Assignment Book (p. 231)

Part 1. Division Practice

Choice of tools may vary.

A. 90; mental math is an appropriate tool

B. 30; mental math is an appropriate tool

C. 2469; paper and pencil are appropriate tools

D. 56; calculators are appropriate tools

E. $100\frac{9}{25}$ or 100 R9; mental math or paper and pencil are appropriate tools.

F. $40\frac{1}{6}$ or 40 R10; mental math, paper and pencil, or calculators are appropriate tools.

Part 2. Fractions, Decimals, and Percents

1. 15 students

2. A. $\frac{8}{15}$ **B.** 0.53   **C.** 53%

3. A. $\frac{24}{32} = \frac{3}{4}$ **B.** 75%

4. Less than 50%; 39% of the students wore baseball caps.

Name _____ Date _____

Unit 16 Home Practice

PART 1 Division Practice
Use an appropriate strategy to find an exact answer for each of the following problems. You can choose between mental math, paper and pencil, and calculators. Mention which tool you used to solve each problem. Estimate to see if your answers are reasonable.

A. 8100 ÷ 90 =   B. 18,000 ÷ 600 =   C. 12,345 ÷ 5 =

D. 40,824 ÷ 729 =   E. 2509 ÷ 25 =   F. 2410 ÷ 60 =

PART 2 Fractions, Decimals, and Percents

1. A group of 18 students from Mr. Moreno's class went to a baseball game; $\frac{5}{6}$ of the students cheered for the home team. How many students cheered for the home team?

2. Blanca brought $15 to the game. She spent $7 on food. The rest of her money she spent on souvenirs.
   A. What fraction of her money did she spend on souvenirs?
   B. Write the fraction in Question 2A as a decimal. Round your answer to the nearest hundredth.
   C. Write the decimal in Question 2B as a percent.

3. The home team has won 24 out of their last 32 games.
   A. What fraction of the games have they won? Write this fraction in lowest terms.
   B. What percentage of their games have they won?

4. Out of the 18 students 7 wore baseball caps to the game. Did more or less than 50% of the students wear a cap? What percentage of the students wore baseball caps? Give your answer to the nearest percent.

BRINGING IT ALL TOGETHER: AN ASSESSMENT UNIT   DAB • Grade 5 • Unit 16 **231**

Discovery Assignment Book - page 231

Discovery Assignment Book (p. 232)

Part 3. Making Brownies

1. 2 squares chocolate, $\frac{3}{8}$ cup butter, $\frac{3}{4}$ cup sugar, 2 eggs, $\frac{1}{2}$ teaspoon vanilla, $\frac{1}{3}$ cup flour, and $\frac{1}{8}$ cup walnuts.

2. 8 squares chocolate, $1\frac{1}{2}$ cups butter, 3 cups sugar, 8 eggs, 2 teaspoons vanilla, $1\frac{1}{3}$ cups flour, and $\frac{1}{2}$ cup walnuts.

Part 4. Geometry

1. $D = 10.2$ cm

2. $C = 25.1$ cm

3. Perimeter = 30 cm

4. Area = 36 sq cm

Name _____ Date _____

PART 3 Making Brownies
Below is a list of ingredients Manny uses to make one batch of walnut crunch brownies.

Walnut Crunch Brownies
4 squares chocolate
$\frac{3}{4}$ cup butter
$1\frac{1}{2}$ cups sugar
4 eggs
1 teaspoon vanilla
$\frac{2}{3}$ cup flour
$\frac{1}{4}$ cup walnuts

1. Manny only has 2 eggs at home. He plans to make half a recipe. List how much of each ingredient he needs.

2. Manny shares his original recipe with Felicia. She plans to double the recipe. How much of each ingredient will she need?

PART 4 Geometry

1. The circumference of a circle is 32 cm. What is the diameter of the circle? Give your answer to the nearest tenth of a centimeter. (Use the [π] key on your calculator or use 3.14 for π.)

2. The radius of a circle is 4 cm. What is the circumference of the circle? Give your answer to the nearest tenth of a centimeter. (Use the [π] key on your calculator or use 3.14 for π.)

3. The length of a rectangle is 6 cm. Its area is 54 sq cm. What is its perimeter?

4. The perimeter of a square is 24 cm. What is the area of the square?

232 DAB • Grade 5 • Unit 16   BRINGING IT ALL TOGETHER: AN ASSESSMENT UNIT

Discovery Assignment Book - page 232

Name _____ Date _____

PART 5 Practice

Solve the following problems using paper and pencil or mental math.
Estimate to be sure your answers are reasonable. Give any remainders
as whole numbers.

1. $63 \times 72 =$ 2. $3089 \times 8 =$ 3. $3090 \div 3 =$

4. $178.24 + 36.8 =$ 5. $0.65 \times 46 =$ 6. $17,346 \div 6 =$

7. $7\frac{7}{8} + 5\frac{2}{3} =$ 8. $\frac{2}{3} - \frac{11}{18} =$

9. $\frac{4}{9} \times \frac{3}{4} =$ 10. $\frac{3}{8} \times 80 =$

BRINGING IT ALL TOGETHER: AN ASSESSMENT UNIT   DAB • Grade 5 • Unit 16 **233**

Discovery Assignment Book - page 233

Discovery Assignment Book (p. 233)

Part 5. Practice

1. 4536
2. 24,712
3. 1030
4. 215.04
5. 29.9
6. 2891
7. $13\frac{13}{24}$
8. $\frac{1}{18}$
9. $\frac{1}{3}$
10. 30

Name _____ Date _____

PART 6 The End of the School Year

Choose an appropriate method to solve each of the following problems. For
some questions you may need to find an exact answer, while for others you
may only need an estimate. For each question, you may choose to use paper
and pencil, mental math, or a calculator. Use a separate sheet of paper to
explain how you solved each problem.

1. On the last day of school Mr. Moreno collected his students' books. If each
   of his 22 students returns all of his or her books, Mr. Moreno should have
   132 textbooks. How many textbooks did each student use during the year?

2. If a student loses a school library book, he or she must pay for the book. If
   the book is returned late, the student must pay a fine of 5¢ a school day
   for every school day it was late. Manny should have returned a book by
   March 25. It is June 2. If the book costs $3.95, is it cheaper for Manny to
   buy the book or return it and pay the overdue fine? Share your strategies.

3. Six students stayed after school to help Mr. Moreno pack up the classroom.
   He treated them to juice and popcorn. If Mr. Moreno bought 6 cans of juice
   from the machine in the teacher's lounge, it would have cost him 50¢ per
   can. Instead, on the way to school he bought six cans of juice for $2.69.
   How much did Mr. Moreno save per can?

4. On the way home, Blanca and Edward stopped at the park to play
   basketball. They both tried to shoot free throws. They both averaged
   2 successful free throws out of 5 tries.
   A. If Blanca tried 20 times, how many free throws did she make?

   B. Edward made 12 free throws. How many times did he try?

5. Mr. Moreno decorated one bulletin board for next fall. Then he covered the
   board with butcher paper, so his decorations wouldn't fade. He has a
   bulletin board that is 2.4 meters long and 1.3 meters wide. What is the area
   of the bulletin board in square meters?

234 DAB • Grade 5 • Unit 16   BRINGING IT ALL TOGETHER: AN ASSESSMENT UNIT

Discovery Assignment Book - page 234

Discovery Assignment Book (p. 234)

Part 6. The End of the School Year

1. 6 textbooks
2. Pay the overdue fines. Strategies will vary.
3. About a nickel per can
4. A. 8
   B. 30
5. 3.12 sq m

Glossary

This glossary provides definitions of key vocabulary terms in the Grade 5 lessons. Locations of key vocabulary terms in the curriculum are included with each definition. Components Key: URG = *Unit Resource Guide* and SG = *Student Guide.*

A

Acute Angle (URG Unit 6; SG Unit 6)
An angle that measures less than 90°.

Acute Triangle (URG Unit 6 & Unit 15; SG Unit 6 & Unit 15)
A triangle that has only acute angles.

All-Partials Multiplication Method (URG Unit 2)
A paper-and-pencil method for solving multiplication problems. Each partial product is recorded on a separate line. (*See also* partial product.)

$$\begin{array}{r} 186 \\ \times\ 3 \\ \hline 18 \\ 240 \\ 300 \\ \hline 558 \end{array}$$

Altitude of a Triangle (URG Unit 15; SG Unit 15)
A line segment from a vertex of a triangle perpendicular to the opposite side or to the line extending the opposite side; also, the length of this line. The altitude is also called the height of the triangle.

Angle (URG Unit 6; SG Unit 6)
The amount of turning or the amount of opening between two rays that have the same endpoint.

Arc (URG Unit 14; SG Unit 14)
Part of a circle between two points. (*See also* circle.)

Area (URG Unit 4 & Unit 15; SG Unit 4 & Unit 15)
A measurement of size. The area of a shape is the amount of space it covers, measured in square units.

Average (URG Unit 1 & Unit 4; SG Unit 1 & Unit 4)
A number that can be used to represent a typical value in a set of data. (*See also* mean, median, and mode.)

Axes (URG Unit 10; SG Unit 10)
Reference lines on a graph. In the Cartesian coordinate system, the axes are two perpendicular lines that meet at the origin. The singular of axes is axis.

B

Base of a Triangle (URG Unit 15; SG Unit 15)
One of the sides of a triangle; also, the length of the side. A perpendicular line drawn from the vertex opposite the base is called the height or altitude of the triangle.

Base of an Exponent (URG Unit 2; SG Unit 2)
When exponents are used, the number being multiplied. In $3^4 = 3 \times 3 \times 3 \times 3 = 81$, the 3 is the base and the 4 is the exponent. The 3 is multiplied by itself 4 times.

Base-Ten Pieces (URG Unit 2; SG Unit 2)
A set of manipulatives used to model our number system as shown in the figure below. Note that a skinny is made of 10 bits, a flat is made of 100 bits, and a pack is made of 1000 bits.

Base-Ten Shorthand (URG Unit 2)
A graphical representation of the base-ten pieces as shown below.

Nickname	Picture	Shorthand
bit		
skinny		
flat		
pack		

Benchmarks (SG Unit 7)
Numbers convenient for comparing and ordering numbers, e.g., 0, $\frac{1}{2}$, 1 are convenient benchmarks for comparing and ordering fractions.

Best-Fit Line (URG Unit 3; SG Unit 3)
The line that comes closest to the points on a point graph.

Binning Data (URG Unit 8; SG Unit 8)
Placing data from a data set with a large number of values or large range into intervals in order to more easily see patterns in the data.

Bit (URG Unit 2; SG Unit 2)
A cube that measures 1 cm on each edge.
It is the smallest of the base-ten pieces and
is often used to represent 1. (*See also* base-ten pieces.)

C

Cartesian Coordinate System (URG Unit 10;
  SG Unit 10)
A method of locating points on a flat surface by means of an ordered pair of numbers. This method is named after its originator, René Descartes. (*See also* coordinates.)

Categorical Variable (URG Unit 1; SG Unit 1)
Variables with values that are not numbers. (*See also* variable and value.)

Center of a Circle (URG Unit 14; SG Unit 14)
The point such that every point on a circle is the same distance from it. (*See also* circle.)

Centiwheel (URG Unit 7; SG Unit 7)
A circle divided into 100 equal sections used in exploring fractions, decimals, and percents.

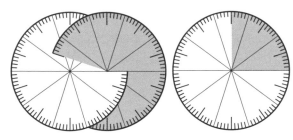

Central Angle (URG Unit 14; SG Unit 14)
An angle whose vertex is at the center of a circle.

Certain Event (URG Unit 7; SG Unit 7)
An event that has a probability of 1 (100%).

Chord (URG Unit 14; SG Unit 14)
A line segment that connects two points on a circle.
(*See also* circle.)

Circle (URG Unit 14; SG Unit 14)
A curve that is made up of all the points that are the same distance from one point, the center.

Circumference (URG Unit 14; SG Unit 14)
The distance around a circle.

Common Denominator (URG Unit 5 & Unit 11;
  SG Unit 5 & Unit 11)
A denominator that is shared by two or more fractions. A common denominator is a common multiple of the denominators of the fractions. 15 is a common denominator of $\frac{2}{3}$ ($= \frac{10}{15}$) and $\frac{4}{5}$ ($= \frac{12}{15}$) since 15 is divisible by both 3 and 5.

Common Fraction (URG Unit 7; SG Unit 7)
Any fraction that is written with a numerator and denominator that are whole numbers. For example, $\frac{3}{4}$ and $\frac{9}{4}$ are both common fractions. (*See also* decimal fraction.)

Commutative Property of Addition (URG Unit 2)
The order of the addends in an addition problem does not matter, e.g., $7 + 3 = 3 + 7$.

Commutative Property of Multiplication (URG Unit 2)
The order of the factors in a multiplication problem does not matter, e.g., $7 \times 3 = 3 \times 7$. (*See also* turn-around facts.)

Compact Method (URG Unit 2)
Another name for what is considered the traditional multiplication algorithm.

$$\begin{array}{r} {}^{2}{}^{1}186 \\ \times\ 3 \\ \hline 558 \end{array}$$

Composite Number (URG Unit 11; SG Unit 11)
A number that has more than two distinct factors. For example, 9 has three factors (1, 3, 9) so it is a composite number.

Concentric Circles (URG Unit 14; SG Unit 14)
Circles that have the same center.

Congruent (URG Unit 6 & Unit 10; SG Unit 6)
Figures that are the same shape and size. Polygons are congruent when corresponding sides have the same length and corresponding angles have the same measure.

Conjecture (URG Unit 11; SG Unit 11)
A statement that has not been proved to be true, nor shown to be false.

Convenient Number (URG Unit 2; SG Unit 2)
A number used in computation that is close enough to give a good estimate, but is also easy to compute with mentally, e.g., 25 and 30 are convenient numbers for 27.

Convex (URG Unit 6)
A shape is convex if for any two points in the shape, the line segment between the points is also inside the shape.

Coordinates (URG Unit 10; SG Unit 10)
An ordered pair of numbers that locates points on a flat surface relative to a pair of coordinate axes. For example, in the ordered pair (4, 5), the first number (coordinate) is the distance from the point to the vertical axis and the second coordinate is the distance from the point to the horizontal axis. (*See also* axes.)

Corresponding Parts (URG Unit 10; SG Unit 10)
Matching parts in two or more figures. In the figure
below, Sides AB and A′B′ are corresponding parts.

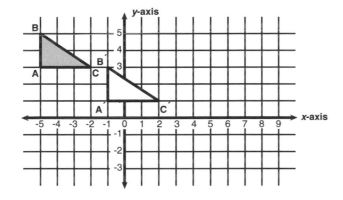

Cryptography (SG Unit 11) The study of secret codes.

Cubic Centimeter (URG Unit 13)
The volume of a cube that is one centimeter long on
each edge.

D

Data (SG Unit 1)
Information collected in an experiment or survey.

Decagon (URG Unit 6; SG Unit 6)
A ten-sided, ten-angled polygon.

Decimal (URG Unit 7; SG Unit 7)
1. A number written using the base ten place value
   system.
2. A number containing a decimal point.

Decimal Fraction (URG Unit 7; SG Unit 7)
A fraction written as a decimal. For example, 0.75 and
0.4 are decimal fractions and $\frac{75}{100}$ and $\frac{4}{10}$ are the equivalent
common fractions.

Degree (URG Unit 6; SG Unit 6)
A degree (°) is a unit of measure for angles. There are
360 degrees in a circle.

Denominator (URG Unit 3; SG Unit 3)
The number below the line in a fraction. The denominator indicates the number of equal parts in which the unit
whole is divided. For example, the 5 is the denominator
in the fraction $\frac{2}{5}$. In this case the unit whole is divided into
five equal parts. (*See also* numerator.)

Density (URG Unit 13; SG Unit 13)
The ratio of an object's mass to its volume.

Diagonal (URG Unit 6)
A line segment that connects nonadjacent corners of
a polygon.

Diameter (URG Unit 14; SG Unit 14)
1. A line segment that connects two points on a circle
   and passes through the center.
2. The length of this line segment.

Digit (SG Unit 2)
Any one of the ten symbols 0, 1, 2, 3, 4, 5, 6, 7, 8, 9.
The number 37 is made up of the digits 3 and 7.

Dividend (URG Unit 4 & Unit 9; SG Unit 4 & Unit 9)
The number that is divided in a division problem,
e.g., 12 is the dividend in 12 ÷ 3 = 4.

Divisor (URG Unit 2, Unit 4, & Unit 9; SG Unit 2,
  Unit 4, & Unit 9)
In a division problem, the number by which another
number is divided. In the problem 12 ÷ 4 = 3, the 4
is the divisor, the 12 is the dividend, and the 3 is the
quotient.

Dodecagon (URG Unit 6; SG Unit 6)
A twelve-sided, twelve-angled polygon.

E

Endpoint (URG Unit 6; SG Unit 6)
The point at either end of a line segment or the point at
the end of a ray.

Equally Likely (URG Unit 7; SG Unit 7)
When events have the same probability, they are called
equally likely.

Equidistant (URG Unit 14)
At the same distance.

Equilateral Triangle (URG Unit 6, Unit 14, & Unit 15)
A triangle that has all three sides equal in length. An
equilateral triangle also has three equal angles.

Equivalent Fractions (URG Unit 3; SG Unit 3)
Fractions that have the same value, e.g., $\frac{2}{4} = \frac{1}{2}$.

Estimate (URG Unit 2; SG Unit 2)
1. To find *about* how many (as a verb).
2. A number that is *close to* the desired number (as a
   noun).

Expanded Form (SG Unit 2)
A way to write numbers that shows the place value of
each digit, e.g., 4357 = 4000 + 300 + 50 + 7.

Exponent (URG Unit 2 & Unit 11; SG Unit 2 & Unit 11)
The number of times the base is multiplied by itself.
In $3^4 = 3 \times 3 \times 3 \times 3 = 81$, the 3 is the base and the
4 is the exponent. The 3 is multiplied by itself 4 times.

Extrapolation (URG Unit 13; SG Unit 13)
Using patterns in data to make predictions or to estimate
values that lie beyond the range of values in the set of
data.

F

Fact Families (URG Unit 2; SG Unit 2)
Related math facts, e.g., 3 × 4 = 12, 4 × 3 = 12,
12 ÷ 3 = 4, 12 ÷ 4 = 3.

Factor Tree (URG Unit 11; SG Unit 11)
A diagram that shows the prime factorization of a number.

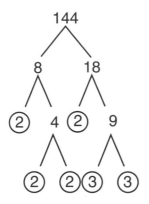

Factors (URG Unit 2 & Unit 11; SG Unit 2 & Unit 11)
1. In a multiplication problem, the numbers that are multiplied together. In the problem $3 \times 4 = 12$, 3 and 4 are the factors.
2. Numbers that divide a number evenly, e.g., 1, 2, 3, 4, 6, and 12 are all the factors of 12.

Fair Game (URG Unit 7; SG Unit 7)
A game in which it is equally likely that any player will win.

Fewest Pieces Rule (URG Unit 2)
Using the least number of base-ten pieces to represent a number. (*See also* base-ten pieces.)

Fixed Variables (URG Unit 4; SG Unit 3 & Unit 4)
Variables in an experiment that are held constant or not changed, in order to find the relationship between the manipulated and responding variables. These variables are often called controlled variables. (*See also* manipulated variable and responding variable.)

Flat (URG Unit 2; SG Unit 2)
A block that measures 1 cm $\times$ 10 cm $\times$ 10 cm. It is one of the base-ten pieces and is often used to represent 100. (*See also* base-ten pieces.)

Flip (URG Unit 10; SG Unit 10)
A motion of the plane in which the plane is reflected over a line so that any point and its image are the same distance from the line.

Forgiving Division Method
(URG Unit 4; SG Unit 4)
A paper-and-pencil method for division in which successive partial quotients are chosen and subtracted from the dividend, until the remainder is less than the divisor. The sum of the partial quotients is the quotient. For example, $644 \div 7$ can be solved as shown at the right.

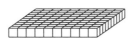

Formula (SG Unit 11 & Unit 14)
A number sentence that gives a general rule. A formula for finding the area of a rectangle is Area = length $\times$ width, or $A = l \times w$.

Fraction (URG Unit 7; SG Unit 7)
A number that can be written as a/b where a and b are whole numbers and b is not zero.

G

Googol (URG Unit 2)
A number that is written as a 1 with 100 zeroes after it (10^{100}).

Googolplex (URG Unit 2)
A number that is written as a 1 with a googol of zeroes after it.

H

Height of a Triangle (URG Unit 15; SG Unit 15)
A line segment from a vertex of a triangle perpendicular to the opposite side or to the line extending the opposite side; also, the length of this line. The height is also called the altitude.

Hexagon (URG Unit 6; SG Unit 6)
A six-sided polygon.

Hypotenuse (URG Unit 15; SG Unit 15)
The longest side of a right triangle.

I

Image (URG Unit 10; SG Unit 10)
The result of a transformation, in particular a slide (translation) or a flip (reflection), in a coordinate plane. The new figure after the slide or flip is the image of the old figure.

Impossible Event (URG Unit 7; SG Unit 7)
An event that has a probability of 0 or 0%.

Improper Fraction (URG Unit 3; SG Unit 3)
A fraction in which the numerator is greater than or equal to the denominator. An improper fraction is greater than or equal to one.

Infinite (URG Unit 2)
Never ending, immeasurably great, unlimited.

Interpolation (URG Unit 13; SG Unit 13)
Making predictions or estimating values that lie between data points in a set of data.

Intersect (URG Unit 14)
To meet or cross.

Isosceles Triangle (URG Unit 6 & Unit 15)
A triangle that has at least two sides of equal length.

Lattice Multiplication
(URG Unit 9; SG Unit 9)
A method for multiplying that
uses a lattice to arrange the
partial products so the digits are
correctly placed in the correct
place value columns. A lattice
for 43 × 96 = 4128 is shown at
the right.

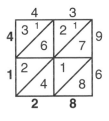

Legs of a Right Triangle (URG Unit 15; SG Unit 15)
The two sides of a right triangle that form the right angle.

Length of a Rectangle (URG Unit 4 & Unit 15;
SG Unit 4 & Unit 15)
The distance along one side of a rectangle.

Line
A set of points that form a straight path extending infi-
nitely in two directions.

Line of Reflection (URG Unit 10)
A line that acts as a mirror so that after a shape is flipped
over the line, corresponding points are at the same distance (equidistant) from the line.

Line Segment (URG Unit 14)
A part of a line between and including two points, called
the endpoints.

Liter (URG Unit 13)
Metric unit used to measure volume. A liter is a little
more than a quart.

Lowest Terms (SG Unit 11)
A fraction is in lowest terms if the numerator and
denominator have no common factor greater than 1.

M

Manipulated Variable (URG Unit 4; SG Unit 4)
In an experiment, the variable with values known at the
beginning of the experiment. The experimenter often
chooses these values before data is collected. The manipulated variable is often called the independent variable.

Mass (URG Unit 13)
The amount of matter in an object.

Mean (URG Unit 1 & Unit 4; SG Unit 1 & Unit 4)
An average of a set of numbers that is found by adding
the values of the data and dividing by the number of
values.

Measurement Division (URG Unit 4)
Division as equal grouping. The total number of objects
and the number of objects in each group are known. The
number of groups is the unknown. For example, tulip
bulbs come in packages of 8. If 216 bulbs are sold, how
many packages are sold?

Median (URG Unit 1; SG Unit 1)
For a set with an odd number of data arranged in order,
it is the middle number. For an even number of data
arranged in order, it is the mean of the two middle
numbers.

Meniscus (URG Unit 13)
The curved surface formed when a liquid creeps up the
side of a container (for example, a graduated cylinder).

Milliliter (ml) (URG Unit 13)
A measure of capacity in the metric system that is the
volume of a cube that is one centimeter long on each
side.

Mixed Number (URG Unit 3; SG Unit 3)
A number that is written as a whole number followed by
a fraction. It is equal to the sum of the whole number and
the fraction.

Mode (URG Unit 1; SG Unit 1)
The most common value in a data set.

Mr. Origin (URG Unit 10; SG Unit 10)
A plastic figure used to represent the origin of a coordinate system and to indicate the directions of the x- and
y- axes. (and possibly the z-axis).

N

N-gon (URG Unit 6; SG Unit 6)
A polygon with N sides.

Negative Number (URG Unit 10; SG Unit 10)
A number less than zero; a number to the left of zero on a
horizontal number line.

Nonagon (URG Unit 6; SG Unit 6)
A nine-sided polygon.

Numerator (URG Unit 3; SG Unit 3)
The number written above the line in a fraction. For
example, the 2 is the numerator in the fraction $\frac{2}{5}$. In this
case, we are interested in two of the five parts. (*See also*
denominator.)

Numerical Expression (URG Unit 4; SG Unit 4)
A combination of numbers and operations, e.g.,
$5 + 8 \div 4$.

Numerical Variable (URG Unit 1; SG Unit 1)
Variables with values that are numbers. (*See also* variable
and value.)

O

Obtuse Angle (URG Unit 6; SG Unit 6)
An angle that measures more than 90°.

Obtuse Triangle (URG Unit 6 & Unit 15; SG Unit 6 & Unit 15)
A triangle that has an obtuse angle.

Octagon (URG Unit 6; SG Unit 6)
An eight-sided polygon.

Ordered Pair (URG Unit 10; SG Unit 10)
A pair of numbers that gives the coordinates of a point on a grid in relation to the origin. The horizontal coordinate is given first; the vertical coordinate is given second. For example, the ordered pair (5, 3) gives the coordinates of the point that is 5 units to the right of the origin and 3 units up.

Origin (URG Unit 10; SG Unit 10)
The point at which the *x*- and *y*-axes intersect on a coordinate plane. The origin is described by the ordered pair (0, 0) and serves as a reference point so that all the points on the plane can be located by ordered pairs.

P

Pack (URG Unit 2; SG Unit 2)
A cube that measures 10 cm on each edge. It is one of the base-ten pieces and is often used to represent 1000. (*See also* base-ten pieces.)

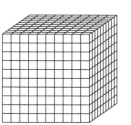

Parallel Lines (URG Unit 6 & Unit 10)
Lines that are in the same direction. In the plane, parallel lines are lines that do not intersect.

Parallelogram (URG Unit 6)
A quadrilateral with two pairs of parallel sides.

Partial Product (URG Unit 2)
One portion of the multiplication process in the all-partials multiplication method, e.g., in the problem 3×186 there are three partial products: $3 \times 6 = \underline{18}$, $3 \times 80 = \underline{240}$, and $3 \times 100 = \underline{300}$. (*See also* all-partials multiplication method.)

Partitive Division (URG Unit 4)
Division as equal sharing. The total number of objects and the number of groups are known. The number of objects in each group is the unknown. For example, Frank has 144 marbles that he divides equally into 6 groups. How many marbles are in each group?

Pentagon (URG Unit 6; SG Unit 6)
A five-sided polygon.

Percent (URG Unit 7; SG Unit 7)
Per hundred or out of 100. A special ratio that compares a number to 100. For example, 20% (twenty percent) of the jelly beans are yellow means that out of every 100 jelly beans, 20 are yellow.

Perimeter (URG Unit 15; SG Unit 15)
The distance around a two-dimensional shape.

Period (SG Unit 2)
A group of three places in a large number, starting on the right, often separated by commas as shown at the right.

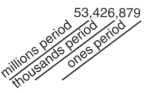

Perpendicular Lines (URG Unit 14 & Unit 15; SG Unit 14)
Lines that meet at right angles.

Pi (π) (URG Unit 14; SG Unit 14)
The ratio of the circumference to diameter of a circle. $\pi = 3.14159265358979....$ It is a nonterminating, nonrepeating decimal.

Place (SG Unit 2)
The position of a digit in a number.

Place Value (URG Unit 2; SG Unit 2)
The value of a digit in a number. For example, the 5 is in the hundreds place in 4573, so it stands for 500.

Polygon (URG Unit 6; SG Unit 6)
A two-dimensional connected figure made of line segments in which each endpoint of every side meets with an endpoint of exactly one other side.

Population (URG Unit 1 Unit 1)
A collection of persons or things whose properties will be analyzed in a survey or experiment.

Portfolio (URG Unit 2; SG Unit 2)
A collection of student work that show how a student's skills, attitudes, and knowledge change over time.

Positive Number (URG Unit 10; SG Unit 10)
A number greater than zero; a number to the right of zero on a horizontal number line.

Power (URG Unit 2; SG Unit 2)
An exponent. Read 10^4 as, "ten to the fourth power" or "ten to the fourth." We say 10,000 or 10^4 is the fourth power of ten.

Prime Factorization (URG Unit 11; SG Unit 11)
Writing a number as a product of primes. The prime factorization of 100 is $2 \times 2 \times 5 \times 5$.

Prime Number (URG Unit 11; SG Unit 11)
A number that has exactly two factors: itself and 1. For example, 7 has exactly two distinct factors, 1 and 7.

Probability (URG Unit 7; SG Unit 1 & Unit 7)
A number from 0 to 1 (0% to 100%) that describes how likely an event is to happen. The closer that the probability of an event is to one, the more likely the event will happen.

Product (URG Unit 2; SG Unit 2)
The answer to a multiplication problem. In the problem $3 \times 4 = 12$, 12 is the product.

Proper Fraction (URG Unit 3; SG Unit 3)
A fraction in which the numerator is less than the denominator. Proper fractions are less than one.

Proportion (URG Unit 3 & Unit 13; SG Unit 13)
A statement that two ratios are equal.

Protractor (URG Unit 6; SG Unit 6)
A tool for measuring angles.

Q

Quadrants (URG Unit 10; SG Unit 10)
The four sections of a coordinate grid that are separated by the axes.

Quadrilateral (URG Unit 6; SG Unit 6)
A polygon with four sides. (*See also* polygon.)

Quotient (URG Unit 4 & Unit 9; SG Unit 2, Unit 4, & Unit 9)
The answer to a division problem. In the problem $12 \div 3 = 4$, the 4 is the quotient.

R

Radius (URG Unit 14; SG Unit 14)
1. A line segment connecting the center of a circle to any point on the circle.
2. The length of this line segment.

Ratio (URG Unit 3 & Unit 12; SG Unit 3 & Unit 13)
A way to compare two numbers or quantities using division. It is often written as a fraction.

Ray (URG Unit 6; SG Unit 6)
A part of a line with one endpoint that extends indefinitely in one direction.

Rectangle (URG Unit 6; SG Unit 6)
A quadrilateral with four right angles.

Reflection (URG Unit 10)
(*See* flip.)

Regular Polygon (URG Unit 6; SG Unit 6; DAB Unit 6)
A polygon with all sides of equal length and all angles equal.

Remainder (URG Unit 4 & Unit 9; SG Unit 4 & Unit 9)
Something that remains or is left after a division problem. The portion of the dividend that is not evenly divisible by the divisor, e.g., $16 \div 5 = 3$ with 1 as a remainder.

Repeating Decimals (SG Unit 9)
A decimal fraction with one or more digits repeating without end.

Responding Variable (URG Unit 4; SG Unit 4)
The variable whose values result from the experiment. Experimenters find the values of the responding variable by doing the experiment. The responding variable is often called the dependent variable.

Rhombus (URG Unit 6; SG Unit 6)
A quadrilateral with four equal sides.

Right Angle (URG Unit 6; SG Unit 6)
An angle that measures 90°.

Right Triangle (URG Unit 6 & Unit 15; SG Unit 6 & Unit 15)
A triangle that contains a right angle.

Rubric (URG Unit 1)
A scoring guide that can be used to guide or assess student work.

S

Sample (URG Unit 1)
A part or subset of a population.

Scalene Triangle (URG Unit 15)
A triangle that has no sides that are equal in length.

Scientific Notation (URG Unit 2; SG Unit 2)
A way of writing numbers, particularly very large or very small numbers. A number in scientific notation has two factors. The first factor is a number greater than or equal to one and less than ten. The second factor is a power of 10 written with an exponent. For example, 93,000,000 written in scientific notation is 9.3×10^7.

Septagon (URG Unit 6; SG Unit 6)
A seven-sided polygon.

Side-Angle-Side (URG Unit 6 & Unit 14)
A geometric property stating that two triangles having two corresponding sides with the included angle equal are congruent.

Side-Side-Side (URG Unit 6)
A geometric property stating that two triangles having corresponding sides equal are congruent.

Sides of an Angle (URG Unit 6; SG Unit 6)
The sides of an angle are two rays with the same endpoint. (*See also* endpoint and ray.)

Sieve of Eratosthenes (SG Unit 11)
A method for separating prime numbers from nonprime numbers developed by Eratosthenes, an Egyptian librarian, in about 240 BCE.

Similar (URG Unit 6; SG Unit 6)
Similar shapes have the same shape but not necessarily the same size.

Skinny (URG Unit 2; SG Unit 2)
A block that measures 1 cm $\times$ 1 cm $\times$ 10 cm.
It is one of the base-ten pieces
and is often used to represent 10.
(*See also* base-ten pieces.)

Slide (URG Unit 10; SG Unit 10)
Moving a geometric figure in the plane by moving every
point of the figure the same distance in the same direction. Also called translation.

Speed (URG Unit 3 & Unit 5; SG Unit 3 & Unit 5)
The ratio of distance moved to time taken, e.g.,
3 miles/1 hour or 3 mph is a speed.

Square (URG Unit 6 & Unit 14; SG Unit 6)
A quadrilateral with four equal sides and four right
angles.

Square Centimeter (URG Unit 4; SG Unit 4)
The area of a square that is 1 cm long on each side.

Square Number (URG Unit 11)
A number that is the product of a whole number multiplied by itself. For example, 25 is a square number since
$5 \times 5 = 25$. A square number can be represented by a
square array with the same number of rows as columns.
A square array for 25 has 5 rows of 5 objects in each row
or 25 total objects.

Standard Form (SG Unit 2)
The traditional way to write a number, e.g., standard
form for three hundred fifty-seven is 357. (*See also*
expanded form and word form.)

Standard Units (URG Unit 4)
Internationally or nationally agreed-upon units used in
measuring variables, e.g., centimeters and inches are
standard units used to measure length and square centimeters and square inches are used to measure area.

Straight Angle (URG Unit 6; SG Unit 6)
An angle that measures 180°.

T

Ten Percent (URG Unit 4; SG Unit 4)
10 out of every hundred or $\frac{1}{10}$.

Tessellation (URG Unit 6 & Unit 10; SG Unit 6)
A pattern made up of one or more repeated shapes that
completely covers a surface without any gaps or overlaps.

Translation
(*See* slide.)

Trapezoid (URG Unit 6)
A quadrilateral with exactly one pair of parallel sides.

Triangle (URG Unit 6; SG Unit 6)
A polygon with three sides.

Triangulating (URG Unit 6; SG Unit 6)
Partitioning a polygon into two or more nonoverlapping
triangles by drawing diagonals that do not intersect.

Turn-Around Facts (URG Unit 2)
Multiplication facts that have the same factors but in a
different order, e.g., $3 \times 4 = 12$ and $4 \times 3 = 12$.
(*See also* commutative property of multiplication.)

Twin Primes (URG Unit 11; SG Unit 11)
A pair of prime numbers whose difference is 2.
For example, 3 and 5 are twin primes.

U

Unit Ratio (URG Unit 13; SG Unit 13)
A ratio with a denominator of one.

V

Value (URG Unit 1; SG Unit 1)
The possible outcomes of a variable. For example, red,
green, and blue are possible values for the variable *color.*
Two meters and 1.65 meters are possible values for the
variable *length.*

Variable (URG Unit 1; SG Unit 1)
1. An attribute or quantity that changes or varies.
   (*See also* categorical variable and numerical variable.)
2. A symbol that can stand for a variable.

Variables in Proportion (URG Unit 13; SG Unit 13)
When the ratio of two variables in an experiment is
always the same, the variables are in proportion.

Velocity (URG Unit 5; SG Unit 5)
Speed in a given direction. Speed is the ratio of the distance traveled to time taken.

Vertex (URG Unit 6; SG Unit 6)
A common point of two rays or line segments that form
an angle.

Volume (URG Unit 13)
The measure of the amount of space occupied by an
object.

W

Whole Number
Any of the numbers 0, 1, 2, 3, 4, 5, 6 and so on.

Width of a Rectangle (URG Unit 4 & Unit 15;
   SG Unit 4 & Unit 15)
The distance along one side of a rectangle is the length
and the distance along an adjacent side is the width.

Word Form (SG Unit 2)
A number expressed in words, e.g., the word form for
123 is "one hundred twenty-three." (*See also* expanded
form and standard form.)

X

Y

Z